Reflect, Evolve, Lead

THE POWER OF METACOGNITION

DR. TEDDY OTT

LUCIDBOOKS

Reflect, Evolve, Lead: The Power of Metacognition

Copyright © 2026 by Dr. Teddy Ott

Published by Lucid Books in Houston, TX
www.LucidBooks.com

All rights reserved. No part of this publication may be reproduced, stored in a retrieval system, or transmitted in any form by any means, electronic, mechanical, photocopy, recording, or otherwise, without the prior permission of the publisher, except as provided for by USA copyright law.

Unless otherwise indicated, scripture quotations are taken from the NIV® Bible (The Holy Bible, New International Version®, NIV®.) Copyright ©1973, 1978, 1984, 2011 by Biblica, Inc.™ Used by permission of Zondervan. All rights reserved worldwide. www.zondervan.com The "NIV" and "New International Version" are trademarks registered in the United States Patent and Trademark Office by Biblica, Inc.™

Scripture quotations marked (ESV) are taken from the ESV® Bible (The Holy Bible, English Standard Version®), copyright © 2001 by Crossway, a publishing ministry of Good News Publishers. Used by permission. All rights reserved.

Scripture quotations marked (KJV) are taken from the King James Version (KJV): King James Version, public domain.

ISBN: 978-1-63296-920-0 (Paperback)
ISBN: 978-1-63296-921-7 (Hardback)
eISBN: 978-1-63296-922-4

Special Sales: Most Lucid Books titles are available in special quantity discounts. Custom imprinting or excerpting can also be done to fit special needs. Contact Lucid Books at Info@LucidBooks.com

To my family, whose love and support have carried me through every season of life, and to the Lord, who has guided my steps and given me the wisdom to lead, teach, and serve. And to the students, teachers, and leaders who inspire me daily to reflect, grow, and lead with purpose.

Contents

Introduction 1

Chapter 1: Defining Metacognition 7

Chapter 2: Higher-Order Thinking and Creativity 17

Chapter 3: Reflective Leadership 29

Chapter 4: Learning to Be Wise 39

Chapter 5: Metacognition as a Catalyst for Lifelong Learning 55

Chapter 6: The Role of Leadership Development 71

Chapter 7: Promoting Self-Regulated Learning 83

Chapter 8: "Evolve" as a Tool for Metacognition 99

Chapter 9: Case Studies and Research: Metacognition
and Impact on Learning Outcomes 111

Chapter 10: Ethical Considerations of Metacognition
in Leadership 123

Chapter 11: Reflect, Evolve, and Lead 137

Chapter 12: Metacognition: Shaping the Future of Learning
and Leadership 147

Chapter 13: Leading Through Metacognition 159

References 169

About the Author 175

Special Thanks

I would like to extend my deepest gratitude to my family for their unwavering encouragement and belief in me throughout this journey. To my colleagues and fellow leaders at Three Way ISD, thank you for inspiring me daily and for modeling the power of reflection and growth in action. Special thanks to the students, teachers, and staff who continue to remind me why the work of leadership and education matters so deeply. I am also grateful for the faith community and mentors who have spoken wisdom into my life, shaping both my character and calling. Finally, to the team at Lucid Books for guiding me through the publishing process with clarity and care—thank you for helping me bring this vision to life.

Introduction

In every journey, there are moments that redefine our path, causing us to pause, reflect, and grow. For me, as a pastor, counselor, and leader, these moments often surfaced in the quiet aftermath of difficult conversations or unexpected challenges within my ministry. In these times, I began to understand the profound value of metacognition—the ability to step back and think about my own thinking. This simple yet transformative practice has shaped my approach to leadership and ministry, guiding me to serve others with greater wisdom, empathy, and intention.

As I reflect on the early days of my ministry, I remember confronting issues that tested both my patience and understanding. I encountered elders and deacons, many of whom had years of experience and wisdom, who held steadfastly to traditional views that often clashed with my vision for the church. My initial response was to feel frustrated and misunderstood. I felt the weight of the responsibility, the pressure to find the "right" solution, and the fear of making a wrong decision. But over time, I realized that these conflicts were not simply problems to be solved; they were opportunities for growth—if only I could see them from a different perspective.

In one such pivotal moment, a conversation with an elder highlighted the tension between tradition and progress. His views, deeply rooted in years of service, seemed to contradict my desire for change. I wanted to implement new programs, reimagine how we engaged with the community, and create a space that was both inviting and relevant. But rather than react impulsively or attempt to prove my point, I took a step back and asked myself, *What's really driving my response here?* By reflecting on my own thought process, I realized that my frustration wasn't just about the disagreement—it was also tied to my own insecurities and eagerness to make a mark in my role as a leader. In recognizing this, I was able to approach the conversation with a newfound humility and openness, acknowledging his perspective while also sharing my vision. The conversation that followed was not just a negotiation but a moment of mutual understanding and growth, one that brought us closer together and created a stronger foundation for our work.

It was in these reflective moments that I began to realize the essence of metacognition. It's not just an academic concept; it's a tool for living and leading with purpose. In my journey, I found that metacognition enabled me to not only respond to challenges more thoughtfully but also align my actions with the deeper values and mission that guide my life. By thinking about my thinking, I could transcend my initial reactions, allowing room for clarity, compassion, and ultimately, transformation.

This practice also became essential in my counseling work, where I often met with individuals carrying heavy burdens—wrestling with pain, doubt, and questions of faith. In these interactions, I had to remind myself to listen fully and to be aware of my own biases and assumptions. One of the most transformative lessons I learned in counseling was that to truly serve others, I needed to stay anchored in humility and self-awareness. When I allowed my own thoughts to settle, creating space to understand and empathize with their struggles,

I found that I could offer guidance that was both sincere and impactful. This kind of mindful reflection not only helped me to be present in each conversation but also deepened the connection and trust I built with those seeking counsel.

As I continued to explore the layers of metacognition, I found myself examining other aspects of my leadership in ministry. The concepts I would later write about in *Changed*, *The Pharisee in You*, and *The Narcissistic Church* emerged from these real-life encounters. In *Changed*, I delved into the process of personal transformation, recognizing that true change doesn't occur overnight. It begins with a deep, reflective look at oneself—at our intentions, motivations, and the subtle biases that often go unnoticed. I came to understand that lasting change is impossible without an honest awareness of our own inner workings, without a willingness to question our assumptions and rethink our patterns.

In *The Pharisee in You*, I confronted the pitfalls of self-righteousness, a trap I found myself slipping into at times, often in the guise of "doing what's right." Metacognition helped me see how easy it is to let pride cloud one's judgment. By reflecting on my thought processes, I was able to recognize when my actions stemmed from a need for control or validation rather than genuine service. This awareness prompted me to lead with humility, resisting the urge to let ego dictate my decisions and instead focusing on the greater purpose of my ministry.

The Narcissistic Church, another extension of this journey, addresses how self-centered motives can subtly influence church culture, from leadership decisions to community engagement. As I reflected on this, I saw moments in my own ministry where I had inadvertently allowed my personal agenda to overshadow the true mission of the church. Metacognition became a tool to recalibrate my focus, ensuring that my actions aligned with a Christ-centered vision rather than a pursuit of personal success. By confronting my own motives and biases, I was able to foster an environment that placed the needs of the congregation at the forefront, empowering others to participate in a mission that went beyond individual ambition.

Through these experiences, I discovered that metacognition is not only a method for improving individual awareness but a pathway to more effective, empathetic leadership. It enables us to cultivate a deeper understanding of our own strengths and limitations, to recognize the impact of our words and actions, and to guide others with intention and integrity. This book, *Reflect, Evolve, Lead*, is an invitation to explore the transformative power of metacognition in your own life—whether as an educator, a leader, a friend, or a lifelong learner.

As you journey through the chapters ahead, you'll find insights drawn from both research and real-life experiences, each woven together to illuminate the power of reflective thinking. In these pages, we'll examine how metacognition can ignite creativity, foster personal growth, and empower leaders to inspire those they serve. We'll explore practical strategies for cultivating a reflective mindset and uncovering the deeper layers of thought that shape our decisions and relationships.

In a world where we are constantly called to make choices—some small, some life-changing—metacognition offers a guiding light. It reminds us to pause, to consider not only what we are doing but *why* we are doing it, and to seek wisdom in the quiet spaces of self-awareness. This practice can open doors to profound transformation, equipping us to navigate the complexities of life with clarity and purpose.

May this book inspire you to embrace metacognition as both a practice and a mindset, leading you toward a future where reflection, growth, and intentional leadership become a natural part of who you are. Together, let us embark on this journey of reflection, evolution, and purposeful leadership, empowered by the limitless potential that lies within each of us.

Chapter 1

Defining Metacognition

Uncovering the Power of "Thinking About Thinking"

"Do not be conformed to this world, but be transformed by the renewal of your mind, that by testing you may discern what is the will of God, what is good and acceptable and perfect."—Romans 12:2 (ESV)

Metacognition—often described as "thinking about thinking"—is the conscious awareness and regulation of one's own thought processes. It is the art of stepping outside our own minds to evaluate the thoughts and beliefs driving our decisions and actions. At its core, metacognition calls us to practice intentionality, allowing us to align our thinking with purpose, growth, and truth.

The Apostle Paul's words in 2 Corinthians 10:5 (ESV) remind us that spiritual growth and renewal begin with examining our thoughts. To "take every thought captive" is a profound expression of metacognitive practice: recognizing when our minds are being led astray, questioning those thoughts, and redirecting them toward God's truth. This is as practical as it is spiritual, touching every area of life, including relationships, leadership, and learning.

A Personal Lesson in Capturing and Redirecting Thoughts

In the dynamic world of leadership, individuals are increasingly called upon to be more than managers or directors; they must be visionaries, reflective thinkers, and catalysts for growth. Whether you're leading a school, a business, a nonprofit, or a ministry, the demands of effective leadership require more than action—they require thoughtful awareness and strategic reflection. At the core of this evolution lies a powerful tool: metacognition, the practice of becoming aware of one's own thought processes, evaluating them, and using that awareness to guide decisions and actions. For leaders across all fields, this means not only understanding what we do, but why we do it—and how we can do it better.

Metacognition, in the context of leadership, becomes the lens through which we examine our practices, decisions, and relationships. It allows us to question assumptions, align our actions with our values, and create systems that foster growth in the people and communities we serve. More than just an intellectual tool, metacognition fosters the emotional intelligence and cultural responsiveness needed to lead diverse organizations with integrity and impact.

The Metacognitive Leadership Cycle

This cycle illustrates the continuous process leaders can follow to improve clarity, purpose, and impact:

- **Awareness:** What am I doing?
- **Reflection:** Why am I doing it?

- **Adjustment:** What will I change?
- **Impact:** What is the effect?

This simple yet powerful framework can guide individual and team decision-making and is a key part of building reflective leadership capacity across any setting—whether in education, business, faith-based ministries, or civic organizations.

As author Peter Drucker once said, "Follow effective action with quiet reflection. From the quiet reflection will come even more effective action." This quote encapsulates the essence of the metacognitive cycle and reminds us that thoughtful leadership requires intentional pauses to consider both the journey and the direction.

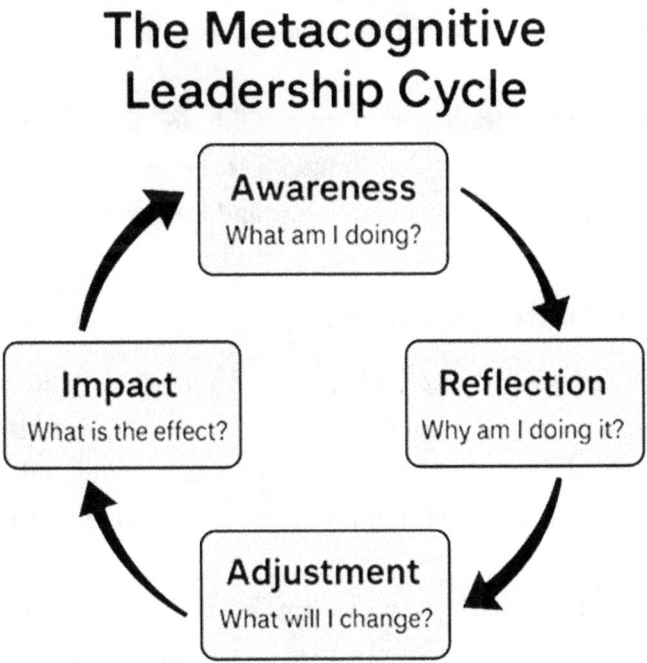

The Foundations of Metacognitive Leadership

John Flavell, who coined the term "metacognition," emphasized its role in learning: The ability to monitor and regulate our cognitive processes is essential for success. For leaders, this translates into reflecting on how we process information, how we solve problems, and how we lead others through change.

Consider a CEO preparing for a company-wide shift in strategic direction. Without reflection, decisions might be reactive, based solely on market pressures or financial forecasts. With metacognition, however, the leader steps back to ask: What assumptions am I making about my team's readiness? How might my communication style influence morale? What are my blind spots? This deeper thinking results in a more thoughtful, effective approach that considers both the human dynamics and the operational needs of the organization.

Whether in education, ministry, healthcare, or industry, leaders who pause to think about their thinking are better equipped to anticipate challenges, respond with empathy, and lead with clarity.

Lessons from History and Life

Throughout history, great leaders have demonstrated the power of metacognitive thinking. Abraham Lincoln famously filled his journals with reflections, revisiting major decisions before acting. His capacity for reflection gave him wisdom, balance, and the foresight to hold a nation together.

In modern leadership, we see similar practices. Visionaries like Satya Nadella of Microsoft emphasize growth mindset and the ability to unlearn and relearn—core components of metacognitive awareness. Nadella writes, "Empathy makes you a better innovator," a concept rooted in the capacity to reflect on one's thoughts and the needs of others.

Even in everyday life, the principle applies. Imagine a parent reflecting on a moment of frustration with their child. Instead of reacting in anger, they pause, consider their emotions, and adjust their response with compassion. That brief pause—the mental checkpoint—is where metacognition changes the outcome.

Abraham Lincoln exemplified metacognitive leadership. Known for his deep self-reflection and disciplined thinking, Lincoln constantly analyzed his own motives, questioned assumptions, and revised his approach. His decision to delay issuing the Emancipation Proclamation until the Union had a strategic victory reveals his inner process: clarity, timing, and deep moral conviction.

He once said, "I am a slow walker, but I never walk back." His commitment to purposeful thought, even under pressure, made him one of history's most effective transformational leaders.

Practical Reflection Tools

Metacognitive leadership is more than theory—it's a practice. Here are tools any leader can adopt:

- **Daily Reflection Log:** Write three things each day: What went well? What didn't? What will I do differently?
- **Weekly Walkthrough:** Review your schedule and ask, "Where did I spend time aligned with my vision? Where did I drift?"
- **Decision Debrief:** After a major choice, jot down your thought process, assumptions, and the results. Revisit after 30 days.

- **Peer Reflection:** Partner with another leader to share a challenge and provide metacognitive feedback—not advice, but questions.

These tools create habits. Over time, they transform reactive leaders into reflective ones, and reflective leaders into transformational ones.

The Inner Life of a Leader

Metacognition also nurtures the inner life of a leader. This is where conviction, purpose, and peace are cultivated. Without reflection, leaders risk becoming mechanical—doing without thinking, moving without meaning.

A wise leader once said, "Leadership begins in solitude. It begins in that inner space where you wrestle with your own heart." That wrestling, that introspective engagement, is metacognition at its deepest level.

In high-stakes roles—whether as pastors, principals, CEOs, or community organizers—this inner clarity provides stability. It keeps leaders aligned with values when faced with opposition. It guards against ego, reactivity, and burnout.

A Culture of Thinking

When leaders model metacognitive habits, they shape the culture around them. Teams learn to think before acting, to question norms, to prioritize meaning over motion. Reflection becomes contagious.

Organizations can build this culture by:

- Starting meetings with "what we learned this week"
- Ending initiatives with structured debriefs

- Embedding reflection into coaching, mentoring, and evaluation systems

Think of an organization as a garden. Without regular tending—reflection—the weeds of confusion, burnout, and misalignment grow fast. But with steady metacognitive care, the garden thrives.

✓ Practical Applications

1. **Practice Reflective Pausing** – Schedule one intentional 10-minute reflection break per day where you ask, "What am I thinking? Why am I thinking this?"
2. **Start a Metacognition Journal** – Record your daily leadership decisions and reflect on the mental process behind them.
3. **Lead Out Loud** – During team meetings, verbalize your thought process behind key decisions to model metacognition.
4. **Use the Pause-Plan-Respond Method** – Teach your team to slow down, think, and then act, rather than react.

✓ Reflection and Renewal

Metacognition reminds us that leadership is not about knowing it all, but about **surrendering our thoughts to Christ.**

> *"We take captive every thought to make it obedient to Christ."* — 2 Corinthians 10:5

Let God renew your mind—not just once, but daily. Reflection isn't optional for a spiritual leader. It is how we partner with God to grow.

✓ Final Thoughts

Leadership is not about perfection. It's about alignment. Metacognition helps leaders realign with purpose, people, and principles. It's not a one-time act—it's a discipline, a rhythm, a way of showing up in the world.

In this chapter, we've defined metacognition, explored its role in diverse leadership settings, and unpacked how reflective thinking can shape not only what we do, but who we become.

The journey forward will build on this foundation—exploring creativity, instructional and strategic leadership, ethical challenges, and personal growth. But it begins here, with a simple but powerful decision:

- To think about our thinking.
- To reflect. To evolve. To lead.

Leadership begins in the mind. When we take time to pause, think about our thinking, and align our thoughts with truth, we lead with greater clarity and compassion.

> **Metacognitive leadership isn't reserved for the intellectual elite—it's the daily work of becoming wise, intentional, and Spirit-led.**

✓ Reflection Questions

1. What patterns of thinking most influence my leadership?
2. How can I better monitor my own internal dialogue during stress or decision-making?
3. What is one area where I need to think more intentionally before acting?

✓ Team Activity – Thinking About Thinking

Objective: Help your team or staff grow in self-awareness and reflection.

1. Ask each member to write down a recent decision they made at work.
2. In pairs, have them explain what led to their decision:
   - What were they thinking?
   - What assumptions were involved?
   - Would they decide differently now?
3. Debrief as a group on what they learned about their thinking patterns.
4. Close with a Scripture or devotional thought from Romans 12:2.

Chapter 2

Higher-Order Thinking and Creativity

"Watch over your heart with all diligence, for from it flow the springs of life."—Proverbs 4:23

As a writer, I've found that metacognition is essential in refining complex ideas and creating original content. In writing *The Narcissistic Church* and *The Pharisee in You*, I had to dive deep into my own experiences and think critically about the theological principles I was exploring. The process of writing these books required me to engage in higher-order thinking—reflecting on the implications of the ideas I was putting forward and considering how my readers would process them. There were moments when I felt the urge to take the easy path and simplify the concepts, but I realized that to communicate the deeper truths I had uncovered, I needed to think more deeply and creatively.

Brené Brown's *Dare to Lead* emphasizes the power of vulnerability in creativity and leadership. She argues that embracing uncertainty and engaging with the discomfort of complex ideas is essential for true innovation. This resonated with me during the writing process, as I had to embrace the discomfort of questioning traditional church practices and explore new ways of leading, challenging myself to think about my thinking to reach new levels of clarity and creativity.

The Artist's Leap: A Story of Higher-Order Thinking and Creativity

Years ago, I met an art teacher named Mr. Jacobs who shared a powerful story about one of his students, Emma. She was a quiet, observant teenager who rarely spoke up in class but had an undeniable talent for sketching. Her work was technically flawless, yet it lacked something intangible—originality. Every project she submitted was an echo of famous pieces she admired. Despite her skill, Emma felt stuck, as though her creativity had plateaued.

One day, Mr. Jacobs challenged her to create a piece entirely from her own imagination. He handed her a blank canvas and gave her a single instruction: "Draw the emotion you've never dared to show."

For weeks, Emma wrestled with the assignment. She stared at the blank canvas, her mind crowded with doubts. Then, one day, it clicked. She thought about how she had always felt overshadowed by her older sister, a star athlete and the family's pride. She realized this feeling of invisibility was the emotion she'd been afraid to confront.

Emma sketched furiously for days, using dark, jagged lines and bursts of unexpected color to capture the tension and sadness she had bottled up for years. The result was raw and unpolished, but it was entirely hers. When she presented the piece, her classmates and even Mr. Jacobs were moved to silence. It wasn't just art; it was her soul on the canvas.

Later, Emma admitted to Mr. Jacobs that the process of creating the piece was transformative. "I had to stop copying what I thought people wanted and start thinking about what I truly felt," she said. "It made me see art—and myself—in a completely new way."

This story reminds us that higher-order thinking often begins with a willingness to embrace discomfort and explore the unfamiliar. For Emma, this meant reflecting deeply on her own emotions and challenging the assumptions that had guided her work. Her breakthrough came not from technical perfection but from her ability to think critically about her own creative process. Emma's journey mirrors the shift from surface-level creativity to true higher-order thinking.

Whether you're an artist, a leader, or an educator, it's this kind of deep reflection that allows us to break through barriers and discover new possibilities.

The Story of the Missing Piece

Years ago, I was counseling a young pastor named David who was struggling with burnout. He felt as though he was pouring his heart into his congregation, yet the ministry seemed stagnant. Attendance was declining, and his sermons, once vibrant, now felt hollow even to him. "I've prayed, studied, and worked harder than ever," he told me, "but something feels . . . off. I'm just going through the motions."

As we talked, it became clear that David had lost sight of the why behind his ministry. His focus had shifted toward external measures of success—attendance, programs, and accolades—rather than the deeper, life-giving work of shepherding souls. His heart, the very wellspring of his purpose, was clouded with distraction.

Together, we engaged in a process of metacognitive reflection. I asked him to step back and think about his thoughts. What assumptions was he operating under? What stories was he telling himself about his ministry? And perhaps most importantly, what was God calling him to prioritize?

After several weeks of prayer and journaling, David had an epiphany. He realized he had been preaching to please rather than preaching to transform. His messages had become safe, carefully crafted to avoid offense, but devoid of the convincing truth he once preached with boldness.

One Sunday, David stood before his congregation and delivered a sermon that was raw and heartfelt. He spoke about his own struggles with pride and his desire to return to authentic ministry. He challenged his congregation to do the same—to reflect on their own hearts and priorities.

The response was overwhelming. People came forward, not because the sermon was polished, but because it was real. David rediscovered his calling not by working harder, but by thinking deeper.

Reflections on Higher-Order Thinking

This story reminds me of the process I went through while writing *The Narcissistic Church* and *The Pharisee in You*. Like David, I had to wrestle with uncomfortable truths—about the modern church, about leadership, and about myself. I had to confront my own assumptions and biases, reflecting on the deeper implications of the ideas I was putting forward.

Higher-order thinking, much like David's journey, requires us to go beyond surface-level solutions. It calls us to analyze, synthesize, and evaluate with diligence, aligning our thoughts with our purpose. This process, though often uncomfortable, is where true creativity and growth are found.

From Creativity to Critical Analysis – Evolving Metacognitive Goals

In the landscape of modern leadership, success is no longer defined solely by knowledge or position, but by the ability to think deeply, creatively, and strategically. Higher-order thinking, encompassing analysis, evaluation, and synthesis, is a hallmark of innovative and adaptive leadership. It allows leaders to go beyond reacting to the present; it empowers them to anticipate the future.

Whether in education, business, ministry, or any organizational context, leaders are responsible for cultivating environments where big-picture thinking, creativity, and problem-solving are not only valued, but practiced. This chapter explores how higher-order thinking shapes leadership impact—and how creativity becomes not a luxury, but a leadership necessity.

Redefining Intelligence: Beyond Routine Leadership

The most effective leaders are not just those who follow instructions or execute plans—they are those who challenge the status quo. They ask why, seek better ways, and imagine new possibilities. This is higher-order thinking in action.

Bloom's Taxonomy, often applied in education, becomes just as relevant in leadership. While lower-order thinking involves remembering and understanding, higher-order thinking involves:

- **Analyzing:** Dissecting problems to understand root causes.
- **Evaluating:** Weighing evidence and determining best courses of action.
- **Creating:** Designing new strategies, systems, and innovations.

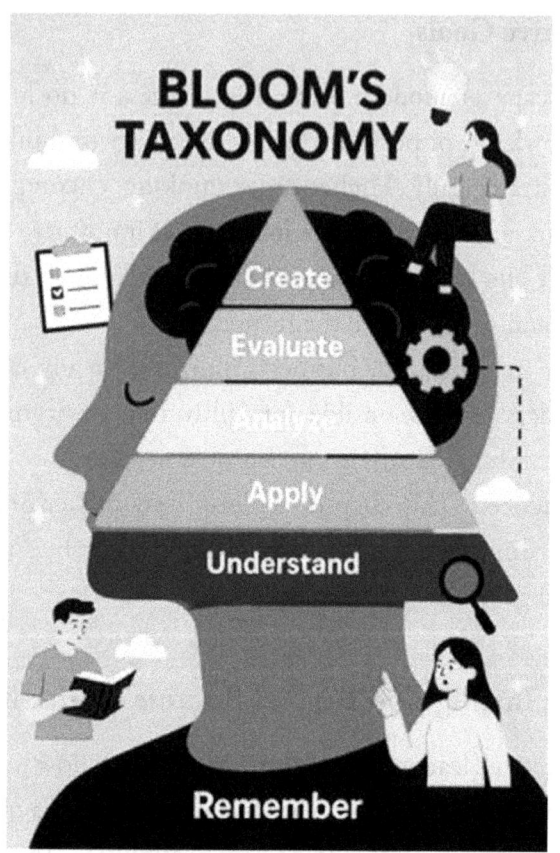

Bloom's hierarchy:

- Remember (policies, procedures)
- Understand (team roles, context)
- Apply (execute strategy)
- Analyze (identify challenges, diagnose barriers)
- Evaluate (review impact, assess culture)
- Create (design new solutions, lead change)

Think of a leader navigating a declining employee engagement score. A surface-level response might involve implementing a few incentives. But a leader engaging in higher-order thinking will dig deeper: What cultural dynamics are at play? How are systems or values contributing to morale? What narratives are being shaped?

The Creative Mindset: Fuel for Visionary Leadership

Creativity in leadership isn't about artistic flair—it's about flexibility, risk-taking, and the ability to generate ideas that move people and organizations forward. Visionary leaders are inherently creative. They:

- See beyond current limitations
- Connect unrelated ideas
- Prototype, iterate, and adapt

Steve Jobs once said, "Creativity is just connecting things." This applies directly to leadership. When we develop creative thinking habits—brainstorming, storyboarding, mind mapping—we access deeper insights and engage others in generative conversations.

A circular graphic with 8 segments:

- Mind Mapping
- Strategic Brainstorming
- Scenario Planning
- Metaphor Thinking
- Reframing Problems
- Creative Debriefs
- Visual Storytelling
- Design Thinking

Organizations that thrive don't just solve today's problems—they invent tomorrow's solutions.

Leadership in the Age of Complexity

We live in a VUCA world—volatile, uncertain, complex, and ambiguous. Higher-order thinking allows leaders to navigate this landscape with clarity and courage. Linear solutions are no longer enough; leaders must think systemically, act iteratively, and adapt continuously.

This is where strategic creativity becomes essential. Consider the leader of a healthcare organization confronting staffing shortages and regulatory changes. By engaging teams in design thinking, brainstorming prototypes, and piloting new workflows, they can reimagine service delivery.

As Margaret Wheatley reminds us, "There is no power for change greater than a community discovering what it cares about." Higher-order thinking, when done in community, fosters movements—not just management.

Practical Applications: Cultivating Higher-Order Thinking in Your Team

To lead with higher-order thinking, leaders must also teach it. Here are methods to embed creative, strategic thinking in your culture:

- **Challenge Assumptions Weekly:** Begin team meetings with "What are we assuming here—and should we?"
- **Use the "What If" Protocol:** Reimagine one process each month using "What if we . . . ?" prompts.
- **Launch Innovation Labs:** Dedicate space/time for teams to experiment with new solutions.
- **Model Vulnerability:** Share your own thought processes and uncertainties to normalize intellectual risk-taking.

- **Mini Case Study:** At a mid-sized nonprofit, the executive director introduced quarterly "reverse mentoring" sessions, where junior staff brainstormed organizational redesign ideas. One session led to a community partnership model that increased reach by 60%. This was higher-order thinking—across hierarchy.

Reflection and Renewal Through Thinking

Leaders often face decision fatigue. One antidote is reflective, creative space. Set aside time weekly to:

- Reframe one current challenge using a metaphor
- Create a mind map of opportunities from a recent failure
- Write a "vision letter" from the future, imagining success three years out

Higher-order thinking doesn't just drive better decisions—it renews the soul. It brings clarity, energy, and possibility.

As Albert Einstein said, "We cannot solve our problems with the same thinking we used when we created them."

Final Thoughts: Lead With Depth and Imagination

Higher-order thinking is not about complexity for its own sake. It's about meaningful depth—the kind that inspires, clarifies, and reimagines. In a world of noise and reaction, leaders who think deeply and creatively become lighthouses of wisdom and innovation.

To think critically is to honor the past. To think creatively is to serve the future. To do both is to lead with power.

Reflection Questions

1. Where in your leadership do you default to surface-level solutions?
2. When was the last time you created something new to solve a challenge?
3. How are you inviting higher-order thinking in your team's daily work?

Leadership Activity: Hold a "Think Tank" hour with your leadership team. Present a challenge, split into small groups, and brainstorm ideas using only questions, metaphors, or sketches. Share out and discuss.

Suggested Reading

- *A More Beautiful Question* by Warren Berger
- *Creative Confidence* by Tom Kelley & David Kelley
- *The Innovator's DNA* by Jeff Dyer, Hal Gregersen & Clayton Christensen
- *Range* by David Epstein

Let us go forward not merely with answers but with better questions, deeper thinking, and a commitment to lead creatively in all that we do.

Chapter 3

Reflective Leadership

Cultivating Growth Through Insight and Faith

"For everything there is a season, and a time for every matter under heaven: a time to be born, and a time to die; a time to plant, and a time to pluck up what is planted . . . He has made everything beautiful in its time."—Ecclesiastes 3:1-2, 11 (ESV)

As we explore the power of higher-order thinking and creativity, we begin to see that leadership isn't just about generating ideas—it's about reflecting on them deeply. The next step in this journey is learning how reflection, grounded in both insight and faith, becomes a catalyst for wise, Spirit-led leadership. In the journey of education and leadership, reflective practice serves as a cornerstone for continuous growth. Reflection enables leaders and educators to assess their actions, refine their methods, and foster personal transformation. In this chapter, we explore the power of reflective practice—how it fuels both metacognitive insight and spiritual alignment—and its profound impact on teaching, leadership, and life.

Reflective leadership has been a cornerstone of my leadership. Early in my career, I faced a conflict between two respected church leaders. The pressure to resolve the issue quickly was intense, but I paused to reflect on my motivations. I realized my instinct to act swiftly stemmed from a fear of division, not from wisdom. In prayer and journaling, I was reminded that true peace is not the absence of conflict but the presence of understanding and truth. This metacognitive pause allowed me to lead with greater clarity, facilitating reconciliation through guided dialogue rather than rushed decisions. In *Dare to Lead*, Brené Brown writes about the importance of staying grounded in our values, even when faced with difficult situations. Reflecting on this principle, I knew I had to lead with integrity and guide both leaders toward reconciliation without compromising the truth.

John Maxwell emphasizes the role of leaders as models of reflective practice. He argues that great leaders don't just take action—they think deeply about their actions and their motivations. By practicing metacognition in this leadership moment, I could approach the conflict with a deeper understanding of the dynamics at play and provide a solution that was both compassionate and effective. This led to a strengthened community and a deeper sense of trust within the church.

More Than Self-Assessment

Reflective leadership is not merely about self-assessment but about cultivating a deep connection between our personal values, our actions, and our spiritual alignment. In my own journey as a leader, I have come to realize that reflection is a transformative process that helps refine decision-making, promotes emotional intelligence, and brings clarity to our calling. This principle is deeply rooted in biblical teachings, where leaders are encouraged to seek wisdom and understanding through reflection.

In the Bible, James 1:5 reminds us, *"If any of you lacks wisdom, let him ask of God, who gives to all liberally and without reproach, and it will be given to him."* Reflective leadership is essentially about positioning ourselves to receive that wisdom, through both our thoughts and actions, in order to grow in our roles and impact others for good.

I remember a season in my leadership where I was faced with a difficult decision about a young teacher in our district. This teacher was passionate, deeply connected with the students, and creative in the classroom, but struggled with consistency and follow-through. Several staff members were frustrated, and parents had started voicing concerns. The easy route would have been to address the issue head-on with immediate corrective action—something decisive that would show the staff and parents I was "on top of things."

But instead of reacting, I chose to pause and reflect. I asked myself: *What is my true goal here?* Was it to quiet the voices of complaint quickly, or was it to nurture growth in a teacher who clearly had potential but needed guidance? Through prayer, journaling, and thoughtful reflection, I realized that my instinct to act quickly came more from pressure to look decisive than from a heart to build lasting change.

This reflection reshaped my response. Instead of delivering a stern directive or rushing into disciplinary action, I invited the teacher into a conversation. I shared the concerns openly but framed them within the bigger picture of their gifts and potential. Together, we created a plan for support, accountability, and mentoring. It wasn't an overnight fix, but over time, the teacher grew into one of the most reliable and impactful educators on our staff.

Looking back, I can see that the turning point wasn't in my words to that teacher—it was in the quiet moments of reflection beforehand. Pausing to examine my motivations allowed me to lead from a place of wisdom rather than pressure. Reflection transformed what could have been a moment of division and discouragement into an opportunity for growth—for both the teacher and me as a leader.

The Greatest Leaders Are the Greatest Followers

Leadership is often seen through the lens of those who command, direct, and envision. Yet, true leadership begins with the ability to follow. The most effective leaders are not those who assert their authority, but those who understand the importance of following with humility and obedience. In fact, the foundation of all great leadership is the ability to follow the guidance of a higher purpose, a calling greater than oneself.

Jesus Christ is the ultimate example of this principle. As the King of Kings, He humbled Himself to follow His Father's will completely. In Mark 10:45, we are reminded, *"For even the Son of Man did not come to be served, but to serve, and to give His life as a ransom for many."* This act of following God's will was not only an act of service but an act of leadership. Jesus' example teaches us that the greatest leaders are those who first understand the power of following God's plan with humility.

The apostle Paul echoes this in Philippians 2:3-5, urging us to embrace the mindset of Christ: *"Do nothing out of selfish ambition or vain conceit. Rather, in humility value others above yourselves, not looking to your own interests but each of you to the interests of the others. In your relationships with one another, have the same mindset as Christ Jesus."*

This scripture shows us that leadership is not about asserting our will but aligning our will with the will of God. A reflective leader recognizes that true leadership stems from submission to God's plan and the willingness to follow His direction with an open heart.

John Maxwell, a renowned leadership expert, aptly said, "A leader is one who knows the way, goes the way, and shows the way." But to truly lead, we must first follow the path that God has laid before us. In other words, we must be followers before we can be true leaders.

Matthew 16:24 presents another critical aspect of leadership and followership: *"Then Jesus said to His disciples, 'Whoever wants to be my disciple must deny themselves and take up their cross and follow me.'"* True leadership requires sacrifice and self-denial. Leaders are not those who demand others to follow them but those who first follow Christ's example of self-sacrifice and obedience. This paradox—being a great leader by being a great follower—defines reflective leadership.

Reflective leadership is rooted in the ability to step back, recognize the bigger picture, and align one's actions with God's calling. Leaders who follow God's lead reflect His love, wisdom, and truth, guiding others not by their own power but by God's strength and direction.

In cultivating reflective leadership, we are called to lead with the same humility and obedience that Jesus showed. By doing so, we empower those we lead to follow with the same faith and trust in God's guidance. Ultimately, this process leads to growth—not just for ourselves but for those who walk beside us.

The Essence of Reflection and Its Role in Growth

Reflective practice is a process of examining our thoughts, evaluating our actions, and understanding our motives. For us as educators and leaders, reflection encourages self-awareness and cultivates a mindset committed to growth and humility. Through reflection, we grow in empathy, make sounder decisions, and ultimately elevate our impact on others. Here are key reasons why reflection is essential for effective leadership and teaching:

- **Personal Growth**: Reflection provides an avenue for personal growth by prompting us to confront our beliefs, biases, and practices. I recall an instance as a principal leading a challenging initiative, where my own reflections revealed a need to create space for my team's input, leading to a more inclusive and empowering environment.

- **Informed Decision-Making**: Reflection enhances decision-making. Reviewing past disciplinary actions, for example, illuminated the need for a proactive, restorative approach to student behavior, promoting understanding and accountability.

- **Empathy and Connection**: Reflective practices help leaders and educators see situations from multiple perspectives. A colleague of mine, a school counselor, reflected deeply on student interactions and recognized underlying mental health challenges, sparking new support programs for those needs.

- **Improved Teaching and Learning**: For educators, reflection on instructional methods can enhance student outcomes. One math teacher, for instance, adapted lessons to include more hands-on activities after realizing that traditional methods weren't resonating with all students, leading to noticeable improvements in engagement and performance.

Approaches to Reflective Practice

Reflective practice can take many forms. Here are some effective methods:

- **Journaling**: A powerful tool, journaling allows us to articulate thoughts, feelings, and observations. With consistent journaling, patterns and growth become visible over time.
- **Peer Collaboration**: Engaging in regular discussions with colleagues fosters shared reflection and provides fresh perspectives.
- **Professional Development Workshops**: These offer tools and techniques for self-assessment, encouraging reflective practice through real-world applications.
- **Feedback Mechanisms**: Soliciting feedback from students, colleagues, and supervisors can reveal blind spots and areas for growth.

Cultivating a Reflective Culture

Leaders can foster a culture of reflection by modeling practices, offering resources, and encouraging open dialogue. Examples include setting aside time for reflective discussions in faculty meetings and celebrating stories of growth. Reflection should be valued as an integral part of the learning environment, benefiting both staff and students.

The Spiritual Foundation of Reflection and Metacognition

Scripture offers a deep well of wisdom on reflection and self-examination. The psalmist's prayer, *"Search me, O God, and know my heart;*

test me and know my anxious thoughts" (Psalm 139:23), is a profound example of reflection as a spiritual practice. This prayer for metacognitive reflection reveals a desire for insight, accountability, and alignment with God's will.

Reflection is not only about refining thought processes but also about nurturing one's spirit and values. Proverbs 4:23— *"Above all else, guard your heart, for everything you do flows from it"*—reminds us that the heart, containing our innermost thoughts and beliefs, is the foundation of our actions. Reflection invites us to refine our thoughts, guard our motives, and align our path with wisdom and purpose.

- **Assessing the Impact of Initiatives**: Reflection allows leaders to evaluate the effectiveness of their actions, identifying areas for improvement and celebrating successes.
- **Reflecting on Difficult Decisions**: By reflecting on challenging choices, leaders can weigh the long-term impacts of their decisions with integrity and humility.
- **Reflection and Leadership as Self-Examination**: Reflecting on one's leadership journey is a discipline that fosters resilience, transparency, and clarity of purpose. As Jesus modeled reflective leadership before choosing His twelve apostles (Luke 6:12-13), leaders today can draw on this example to pause, seek wisdom, and align their actions with their values.

Practical Applications of Reflection in Leadership

Incorporating reflective practice into daily routines enhances thoughtful decision-making and personal growth. Here are a few ways to make reflection a regular part of leadership:

- **Journaling**: Writing down experiences, thoughts, and lessons learned helps leaders recognize patterns and make adjustments in their approach.

- **Seeking Feedback**: Reflecting on feedback, even when challenging, enables leaders to grow in humility and effectiveness.

- **Intentional Pausing**: Setting aside moments of stillness—whether through devotions, walks, or retreats—refreshes perspective and refocuses on values and goals.

- **Reflective Questioning**: Asking guiding questions such as "Am I leading in alignment with my values?" and "How can I serve others through my decisions?" ensures actions remain rooted in integrity and purpose.

- **Prayer and Meditation**: For leaders of faith, prayer offers a time to seek wisdom from God. As Proverbs 3:5-6 advises, *"Trust in the Lord with all your heart . . . and he will make your paths straight."* Reflecting through prayer aligns decisions with divine wisdom.

Reflection as a Path to Integrity and Lasting Impact

Reflection builds strength in both leaders and educators, fostering wisdom, resilience, and authenticity. The habit of learning from every experience, recognizing both successes and mistakes, and refining one's approach cultivates a foundation of integrity and trust. Reflective leaders create environments where team members feel valued, respected, and supported.

James 1:5 encourages us, *"If any of you lacks wisdom, let him ask God, who gives generously."* This invitation shows that reflection and growth are ongoing practices, open to anyone willing to seek wisdom and embrace the journey. For leaders, reflective practices cultivate honesty and openness, allowing them to inspire others by leading with transparency and trustworthiness.

Conclusion: Embracing Reflection as a Path to Wisdom and Transformation

Reflective practice, deeply rooted in both metacognitive awareness and spiritual insight, encourages educators and leaders to prioritize inner growth and continuous improvement. In a fast-paced world that often emphasizes speed and results, reflection calls us to pause, to look inward, and to seek understanding. By embracing reflection, we strengthen self-awareness, enhance relationships, and contribute meaningfully to the lives we touch.

As we make reflective practices a habit, we become better equipped to navigate life and leadership with wisdom and purpose. Let us commit to this journey of thoughtful self-examination, fulfilling our call to lead with integrity, inspire others, and, ultimately, make a lasting impact.

Chapter 4

Learning to Be Wise

Building Deeper Thought Processes

"By wisdom a house is built, and through understanding it is established." —Proverbs 24:3

Reflective leadership opens the door to deeper wisdom. Once we learn to slow down, examine our actions, and realign with God's direction, we begin to build leadership that lasts. The next chapter explores what it truly means to *build wisdom* into our leadership approach, creating structures that support thoughtful, sustainable growth.

Wisdom is not the same as intelligence. It's deeper than strategy, more grounded than knowledge, and more enduring than instinct. It's what allows leaders to navigate complexity with grace, build systems that last, and remain steady when everything around them shifts.

Wise leadership is reflective, deliberate, and rooted in **deeper thought processes**, not just quick reactions or clever ideas.

This chapter explores what it means to build your leadership on wisdom, developing structures that support growth, using insight to drive sustainable change, and fostering clarity that strengthens others.

In today's world, where information is abundant and technology pervades every aspect of life, the ability to think deeply, reflectively, and wisely has never been more critical. Wisdom-based learning—an approach that prioritizes ethical judgment and the consideration of multiple perspectives—is not merely an ideal; it is essential for navigating the complexities of modern existence. As we grow and develop in our understanding, we must remember that we are called to cultivate not only our knowledge but also our moral compass and critical thinking skills.

In my role as an educational leader, I encountered a decision that tested my ability to navigate complex situations. I was tasked with leading the implementation of a new curriculum in the church's education program, which required significant changes. It was an initiative that involved teachers, students, and families, and I knew that wisdom would be key. Reflecting on past experiences and the lessons I had learned helped me see that wisdom wasn't about having all the answers upfront but about being willing to listen, reflect, and collaborate.

In *The 5 Levels of Leadership*, John Maxwell discusses how leaders must evolve through different stages of leadership. At the higher levels, leaders rely on their wisdom, which comes from the reflection of past experiences. By thinking critically about the steps we had taken before and the challenges ahead, I could make decisions that were grounded in experience and guided by a broader vision.

With the advent of artificial intelligence (AI), we now have powerful tools at our disposal to aid in the development of wisdom alongside knowledge. AI applications, particularly scenario-based simulations and ethical decision-making tools, encourage reflective thinking and enable users to evaluate their actions from various angles. This aligns perfectly with my view of reflective thinking as a vital process for making choices that serve the greater good.

The Role of Wisdom in Learning and Decision-Making

Wisdom transcends mere knowledge; it encompasses the thoughtful application of what we know. According to psychologist Robert Sternberg, "Wisdom involves using one's knowledge and experience for the good of oneself and others." In education and professional development, this means nurturing critical thought processes that guide individuals toward ethical and well-rounded choices.

Wisdom is rooted in empathy, foresight, and ethical reasoning—skills that are increasingly vital in a world shaped by AI and automation. Artificial Intelligence (AI) can promote metacognition—or serve as a powerful tool for metacognitive development—in both learners and leaders by facilitating self-awareness, reflection, and intentional decision-making. Here's how:

🔍 1. AI as a Mirror: Promoting Self-Awareness

Artificial Intelligence, when used intentionally, can act like a mirror, helping us recognize patterns in our thinking. For example, an AI writing assistant might flag unclear ideas in a document, prompting the writer to rethink their approach. In leadership, this type of feedback can support wise, data-informed decisions—without replacing the need for human discernment. AI doesn't replace reflection; it enhances it, like a flashlight in a dark room, revealing what we might otherwise miss.

Three core ways AI supports wisdom-based leadership:

- **Clarifying Thought** – via feedback and journaling tools.
- **Simulating Scenarios** – allowing leaders to reflect on complex choices.
- **Promoting Perspective-Taking** – through data and diverse input.

📌 *Example: A student using an AI writing assistant can reflect on sentence clarity and coherence, improving not just the product but their approach to writing.*

2. Scaffolding Metacognitive Strategies

AI can guide users through metacognitive practices such as:

- **Goal Setting:** Tools prompt users to define their objectives before beginning tasks.
- **Planning and Monitoring:** AI-driven checklists or planning apps can help break down tasks and monitor progress.
- **Reflection Prompts:** AI chatbots or journaling tools can pose reflective questions after lessons, meetings, or personal experiences.

📌 *Example: An AI-powered study coach might ask, "What strategy did you use for this problem? Was it effective?"—nudging the user toward deeper awareness.*

📈 3. Personalized Learning & Feedback

AI analyzes patterns in user behavior and adjusts instruction or prompts accordingly:

- Adapts to the learner's cognitive strengths and weaknesses.
- Offers real-time insights into learning gaps and habits.
- Encourages metacognitive thinking by showing trends over time.

📌 *Example: In platforms like DreamBox or Khan Academy, AI adapts problems to student performance, prompting them to consider different strategies.*

🔄 4. AI-Assisted Reflection for Leaders

For leaders and professionals, AI tools:

- Generate insights from large data sets (surveys, feedback, outcomes), helping them reflect on decisions.
- Provide simulations or scenario analysis for decision-making practice.
- Assist in journaling or coaching (e.g., using AI to log leadership decisions and later reflect on them).

📌 *Example: An AI dashboard that visualizes teacher performance data can prompt school leaders to reflect on instructional trends and leadership decisions.*

💬 5. Chatbots and Dialogue Agents for Reflective Thinking

Conversing with AI can:

- Encourage articulation of thoughts (externalizing inner thinking).
- Provide Socratic questioning that deepens reasoning.
- Serve as a "thinking partner" for planning or evaluating decisions.

📌 *Example: A teacher might use ChatGPT to draft a lesson, reflect on student needs, and revise plans in real time based on thoughtful conversation.*

⚖️ 6. AI in Metacognitive Skill Assessment

AI can analyze written reflections, discussion logs, or problem-solving behaviors to assess:

- Depth of metacognitive engagement.
- Quality of strategy use.
- Shifts in cognitive control over time.

📌 *Example: AI might assess journal entries or project logs for evidence of planning, monitoring, and evaluating behaviors.*

AI doesn't replace human reflection—it **augments it**. When designed and used intentionally, AI becomes a **metacognitive companion**, helping students, educators, and leaders reflect on their decisions, adjust strategies, and grow in self-awareness.

As we engage with AI technologies, we can cultivate wisdom in interactive and reflective ways. For instance, scenario-based simulations can present ethical dilemmas and encourage learners to weigh their choices carefully. One notable example is the Moral Machine, developed by MIT, which allows users to explore the moral decisions faced by autonomous vehicles. This tool prompts users to consider different outcomes, helping them practice wisdom in a safe, structured environment where they can receive feedback and insights.

AI Applications in Wisdom-Based Learning

AI applications in education are evolving from mere knowledge delivery to fostering wise and ethical decision-making. Here are several examples of how these tools can encourage deeper thought:

1. **Scenario-Based Simulations**: AI-powered simulations immerse students in complex, real-world situations that demand thoughtful decision-making. For example, the educational game Civics 101 allows students to assume roles like legislators, where they face dilemmas such as deciding between funding environmental programs or public safety initiatives. The AI provides context and insights into the implications of their choices, promoting a comprehensive understanding of the issues at hand.

2. **Ethical Decision-Making Tools**: AI-driven ethical decision-making tools present moral dilemmas that guide users through reflection and critical evaluation. In institutions like Johns Hopkins University, students encounter ethical scenarios that challenge them to prioritize patients in limited-resource situations. The AI assists in considering multiple factors, prompting learners to assess their values and

make well-reasoned decisions, thereby developing a robust ethical framework.

3. **Multiple-Perspective Analysis**: AI can facilitate learning through modeling wisdom via multiple-perspective analysis. In educational settings, AI platforms can present case studies requiring students to examine situations from different viewpoints. For example, in a history lesson, students might explore a conflict by analyzing narratives from both sides. This fosters empathy and encourages careful evaluation of complex issues, essential components of wise thinking.

In the workplace, AI tools can aggregate and present diverse data on intricate matters, prompting leaders to adopt a broader perspective before making decisions. For instance, project management software like Trello employs AI to offer insights from team members with varied expertise, encouraging managers to consider diverse viewpoints and fostering a culture of inclusivity.

Case Studies: AI and Wisdom in Action

To illustrate the impact of AI in fostering wisdom, consider these case studies:

- **Law Enforcement Training**: AI-driven simulators are employed in police academies to create high-stakes scenarios, such as conflict de-escalation exercises. These simulations challenge officers to make quick decisions under pressure and provide real-time feedback on the ethical dimensions of their actions. After each simulation, AI tools guide trainees through reflective debriefings, asking them to consider the ethical implications of their choices.

- **Corporate Leadership Programs**: Organizations like Cisco utilize AI-based decision-making tools to train leaders in ethical and strategic thinking. By presenting business dilemmas with multiple perspectives, AI encourages leaders to consider the long-term effects of their actions and fosters a broader, more inclusive approach to decision-making.
- **Medical Training**: Medical schools employ AI simulations that replicate emergency scenarios, demanding split-second decisions. Following these exercises, AI tools guide students through reflective questions about patient outcomes, team communication, and ethical responsibilities. This practice reinforces wise decision-making and prepares students for real-world challenges with empathy and judgment.

Reflective Thinking and Wisdom-Based Learning

Reflective thinking is an essential component of wisdom, requiring individuals to pause, review their actions, and assess the implications of their choices. I emphasize that "wisdom often emerges when we take the time to consider our decisions deeply." This process helps connect our choices to potential outcomes and cultivates mindfulness, preventing impulsive actions and encouraging well-considered decisions.

AI can bolster reflective thinking by prompting users to evaluate their choices and decision-making processes. For instance, AI in educational contexts might ask reflective questions like, "What were the reasons behind your decision?" or "How would you approach this differently next time?" These prompts guide learners to engage in self-evaluation, a critical habit for internalizing lessons and refining their approaches for the future.

The Trellis and the Vine – A Personal Leadership Reflection

Recently, while working on this very book, I was personally confronted with a hard truth:

> *"Knowing what needs to be done is not the same as implementing it wholeheartedly."* —Dr. Teddy Ott

I want to share something deeply personal—a moment of reckoning that came not in front of an audience or a boardroom, but in quiet reflection while writing this book.

As I wrestled through these chapters—calling leaders to clarity, reflection, and excellence—I realized a sobering truth: **understanding the right path means little if we lack the courage and discipline to walk it.**

That realization was humbling.

You see, I've always carried a deep burden to lead well—to cast vision, set direction, and help others grow. But in the stillness of reflection, I had to admit something I didn't want to face: There have been moments when I offered expectations without follow-through, standards without systems, and encouragement without tangible support.

And that's not the kind of leader I want to be.

That's not the kind of shepherd God has called me to be.

I've spent time asking hard questions—about myself, my leadership, and the impact I want to leave. In that process, one image kept coming to mind that brought deep clarity and conviction: **the trellis and the vine.**

In a vineyard, the **vine** is everything that's alive—growing, stretching, bearing fruit. That's the mission. The people. The relationships. The learning. The life-changing work.

But the vine can't flourish on its own. It needs something to hold it up, to train it, to shape its direction. That's the **trellis**—the structure. The systems. The communication. The framework.

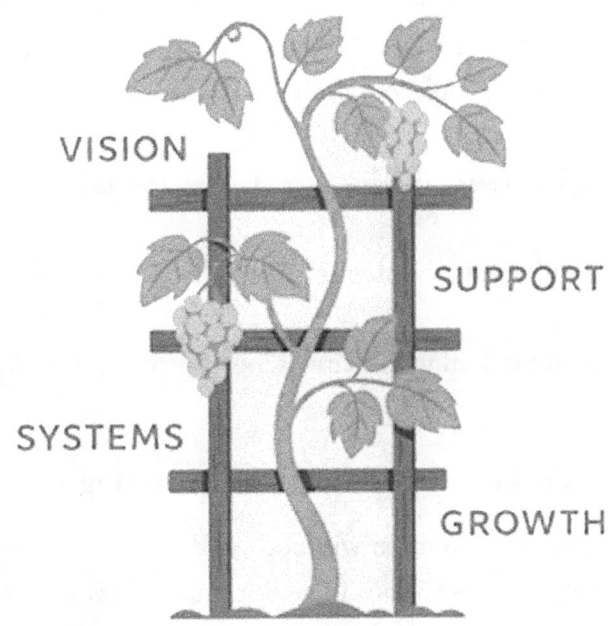

And here's what I've realized: For far too long, I've poured my heart into the vine—because that's where the passion is. But I haven't always built the trellis with the same commitment. At times, I assumed passion would carry the mission. It won't. **Purpose needs structure. Vision needs clarity. Growth needs support.**

And when those supports are missing? Even the strongest vines wither. Intentions turn into confusion. Teams drift. Burnout creeps in.

That truth cut me deeply—but it also woke me up.

So, here is what I want you to know:

I'm not just reflecting—I'm rebuilding.

Not just in philosophy, but in practice. Not just in ideals, but in action.

We're going to build systems that serve and support, not suffocate.

We're going to pursue clarity over confusion, unity over uncertainty, consistency over chaos. Because I believe the vine we're nurturing—our work, our people, our calling—is worth everything it takes to build the trellis that can hold it.

I don't write this as a declaration of failure. I write it as a testimony of grace.

God doesn't just reveal our gaps—He offers wisdom to fill them.

And I intend to lead with that wisdom, every step forward.

Wisdom as the Foundation for Future Learning

AI applications that promote wisdom-based learning are transforming how we approach decisions in education and beyond. These tools encourage individuals to look beyond immediate results, preparing them to act responsibly in an increasingly complex world. By providing structured environments for exploring challenging scenarios, AI serves as a partner in the pursuit of wisdom, aligning with my vision for thoughtful and reflective learning.

In an age where our decisions can have far-reaching implications, wisdom is an essential skill. As we embrace AI-guided exercises and reflective practices, we can empower ourselves and others to make ethical, well-rounded choices.

How Do We Learn?

Learning is a lifelong journey where we set goals, select strategies, evaluate our progress, and adjust our paths. This cyclical process reminds us that we are all, at heart, lifelong learners. Whether as teachers, leaders, or students, we are continually called to self-reflection and improvement. Metacognition, or "thinking about thinking," is central to this journey, guiding us to engage in self-assessment, set intentional goals, and make adjustments as necessary.

In education, this reflective process resonates with the concept of sanctification—a spiritual journey of being set apart for a higher purpose. Both metacognition and sanctification aim to foster growth and development. As leaders and mentors, we aspire to equip our students for their unique roles and callings. Educational researcher John Hattie states, "Teaching metacognitive strategies has one of the highest impacts on student achievement," guiding learners to move beyond rote learning toward deeper understanding.

The Role of Metacognition in Learning Transfer

Metacognition plays a crucial role in enabling students to transfer knowledge across various contexts. Those with strong metacognitive skills can draw connections between different subjects and experiences, recognizing when and how to apply previously acquired knowledge in new situations. This adaptability enhances their problem-solving abilities.

For example, a student who has learned statistical analysis in math class may successfully apply those skills to a social science project requiring data interpretation. This ability to transfer learning is increasingly vital in a world where interdisciplinary knowledge is essential.

A Story of Wisdom in Action: The Decision that Changed Everything

Several years ago, I was faced with a decision that, at the time, seemed like a simple choice but, in hindsight, had profound ramifications. It occurred in a time of great change for the church community I was leading. We had been struggling with the challenge of updating our youth ministry's teaching approach. The old curriculum had been in place for years, and though it had served us well, it no longer seemed to meet the needs of our rapidly changing society. We needed something more engaging, more relevant, something that would connect the youth of our congregation to the timeless truths of Scripture in a way that resonated with their hearts and minds.

The pressure to make the right decision was immense. I knew that the wrong choice could alienate the very people I had been called to serve, and yet, I also felt the weight of the responsibility to guide the ministry in a direction that honored both tradition and progress. It was a delicate balance, and I struggled with doubt and uncertainty.

As I prayed and reflected on the decision, I sought wisdom. I spent hours consulting with fellow leaders and speaking with parents, teachers, and students to understand their perspectives. I didn't rush to a conclusion. Instead, I took time to listen and observe, knowing that wisdom would come through a process of reflection and collaboration.

One evening, as I was reviewing the feedback from a parent meeting, I remembered a lesson from an old mentor of mine. He had always said that wisdom is not about having all the answers upfront; it's about asking the right questions and being open to the possibility that your own understanding might need to change. That was the key: openness. Openness to new ideas, to the voices of others, and to God's direction.

After much prayer and deliberation, I decided to choose a new curriculum—one that integrated more interactive elements, fostered critical thinking, and placed greater emphasis on real-world application. But it wasn't just about choosing a new program; it was about creating an environment where everyone involved, from the youth to the teachers to the parents, felt heard, valued, and included in the process. I didn't simply implement the change; I led with a spirit of collaboration, ensuring that the transition was one of shared purpose rather than top-down imposition.

The change was not without challenges, of course. There were moments of resistance, moments when I questioned whether we had made the right choice. But, in time, the impact of that decision became clear. The youth ministry grew not only in numbers but, more importantly, in depth. Students were more engaged with the material, and the teaching staff found new energy in their work. It was a turning point—a moment when I realized that wisdom wasn't just about knowing the right path; it was about taking the time to seek guidance, to reflect, and to act in a way that honored the wisdom of others while trusting in God's ultimate plan.

Looking back, I see now that the decision was not just about implementing a new curriculum. It was about trusting in the process of reflection, seeking wisdom from multiple perspectives, and applying the knowledge gained to a real-world challenge. The decision shaped the direction of the ministry for years to come and reminded me of the powerful role that wisdom plays in every aspect of life.

It was at that moment that I understood deeply what Proverbs 3:5-6 means: *"Trust in the Lord with all your heart and do not lean on your own understanding; in all your ways acknowledge Him, and He will make your paths straight."* My path wasn't straight because I had all the answers, but because I had the wisdom to trust God and the courage to seek counsel from others, listening to their perspectives and allowing those voices to shape the decision.

That decision, born out of deep reflection and collaboration, became a pivotal moment not just in my leadership journey but in my understanding of what it truly means to lead with wisdom. It taught me that wisdom isn't just about knowing what to do; it's about knowing when to listen, when to trust others, and when to move forward in faith.

Conclusion

In conclusion, wisdom-based learning transcends mere knowledge acquisition; it is about cultivating the capacity to apply that knowledge thoughtfully, ethically, and reflectively. As we navigate the complexities of modern life, the ability to think deeply, empathize with others, and make well-considered choices is invaluable. Through AI applications and reflective practices, we can foster wisdom in education and beyond, empowering individuals to become not just knowledgeable but also wise leaders and decision-makers for the future.

Chapter 5

Metacognition as a Catalyst for Lifelong Learning

"The good man out of the good treasure of his heart brings forth what is good; and the evil man out of the evil treasure brings forth what is evil; for his mouth speaks from that which fills his heart."—Luke 6:45

In the journey of lifelong learning, metacognition serves as a powerful catalyst, encouraging individuals to become more aware of their thought processes and learning strategies. This awareness is crucial in an age characterized by rapid change and evolving challenges. Metacognition allows us not only to acquire knowledge but to reflect on how we learn, making adjustments that enhance our understanding and growth.

As a pastor and writer, I have always believed in the importance of lifelong learning. I remember a time when a congregant came to me, feeling overwhelmed by her struggles with faith. Instead of offering quick solutions, I reflected on my own spiritual growth and how I had learned from my own times of doubt. Through metacognitive reflection, I was able to guide her to see her struggles as part of the learning process rather than obstacles to her growth.

John Maxwell frequently speaks about the importance of continuous personal growth. He believes that leadership is a lifelong journey of learning and improvement. By reflecting on my own growth as a pastor and a leader, I was able to recognize that even in moments of difficulty, there are lessons to be learned. This mindset fueled my commitment to lifelong learning and allowed me to better support those I serve.

The Essence of Metacognition

Metacognition refers to the knowledge and awareness of one's cognitive processes, encompassing two key components: metacognitive knowledge and metacognitive regulation. Metacognitive knowledge includes what individuals know about their own thinking and learning styles, while metacognitive regulation refers to the ability to manage and control these processes during learning tasks.

John Flavell, a pioneering psychologist who coined the term metacognition, emphasized its significance in effective learning: "Metacognition is knowledge about when and how to use particular strategies for learning or problem-solving." For example, consider a high school student preparing for college entrance exams. Through trial and error, they might discover that summarizing material in their own words helps them retain information better than passive reading. This realization leads them to prioritize note-taking as a study strategy, ultimately enhancing their learning experience.

Fostering metacognitive skills allows individuals to reflect on their learning experiences, evaluate their understanding, and adapt their strategies accordingly. This self-regulation enhances academic performance and cultivates a mindset of continuous improvement and adaptation.

> "*Leadership and learning are indispensable to each other.*"—John F. Kennedy

The Connection between Metacognition and Lifelong Learning

Lifelong learning is not merely about acquiring knowledge; it's about cultivating the ability to learn continuously throughout one's life. Metacognition plays a vital role in this process by enabling learners to:

1. **Set Goals**: Metacognitive individuals excel at setting specific, measurable, attainable, relevant, and time-bound (SMART) goals. For instance, an aspiring musician who sets a goal to learn a new instrument within six months can break this down into weekly practice schedules. By tracking progress and adjusting their approach, they remain motivated and focused.

2. **Monitor Progress**: Regularly assessing their understanding and performance allows metacognitive learners to identify areas that require additional focus. For example, a university student studying for a final exam might take practice tests to evaluate their knowledge, enabling them to pinpoint weak points and adjust their study plan accordingly. As philosopher John Dewey noted, "We do not learn from experience . . . we learn from reflecting on experience."

3. **Adjust Strategies**: The ability to modify learning strategies based on self-reflection allows learners to optimize their

efforts. A professional studying for a certification might discover that group study sessions help them grasp complex concepts more effectively than solitary study. By recognizing this, they adjust their strategy and seek collaborative opportunities, enhancing their understanding.

4. **Cultivate Resilience**: Lifelong learners equipped with metacognitive skills are more likely to persevere in the face of setbacks. They understand that challenges are opportunities for growth. As psychologist Carol Dweck states, "A growth mindset is the belief that you can improve with effort." This mindset reinforces their commitment to self-improvement, much like athletes who learn from failures and use them as stepping stones to future successes.

Real-Life Examples of Metacognition in Action

To illustrate the impact of metacognition in fostering lifelong learning, consider these examples:

- **The Artist's Journey**: A painter who initially struggles with color blending takes the time to reflect on their techniques after each session. By observing which colors work well together and which do not, they refine their approach over time. This self-reflective practice leads to greater mastery of their craft and personal growth as an artist.

- **The Business Leader**: A manager at a startup regularly reviews the outcomes of team projects. After a significant setback, they gather the team to reflect on what went wrong and what could have been done differently. By encouraging open dialogue and reflection, the team learns valuable lessons that enhance their future performance and collaboration.

- **The Educator's Evolution**: A teacher dedicates time at the end of each week to reflect on their lessons. They assess which strategies engaged students and which fell flat, using this information to adapt their teaching methods. This continuous self-evaluation not only improves their effectiveness as an educator but also models the importance of metacognition for their students.

- **The Lifelong Learner**: An individual who loves to travel takes note of their experiences in a journal. After each trip, they reflect on what they learned about different cultures and themselves. This practice deepens their appreciation for diverse perspectives and enhances their overall understanding of the world.

Real-Life Example – Benjamin Franklin

Franklin was more than an inventor—he was a disciplined lifelong learner. He created a chart to track personal virtues, reflected daily on his habits, and wrote extensively about what he learned. His famous "13 Virtues" chart is one of the earliest examples of a **self-regulated learning system**. He didn't just want to know more—he wanted to **become better**.

> *"Without continual growth and progress, such words as improvement, achievement, and success have no meaning."*— Benjamin Franklin

Modern Example – Maya Angelou

The late Dr. Maya Angelou, renowned poet and civil rights leader, was a woman who evolved continuously. She said, "Do the best you can until you know better. Then when you know better, do better."

That's metacognition in motion.

Angelou didn't view learning as a classroom experience. She viewed it as **moral and personal growth**—an ongoing journey of evaluating self and society and responding with courage and grace.

Visual Metaphor – The Spiral of Growth

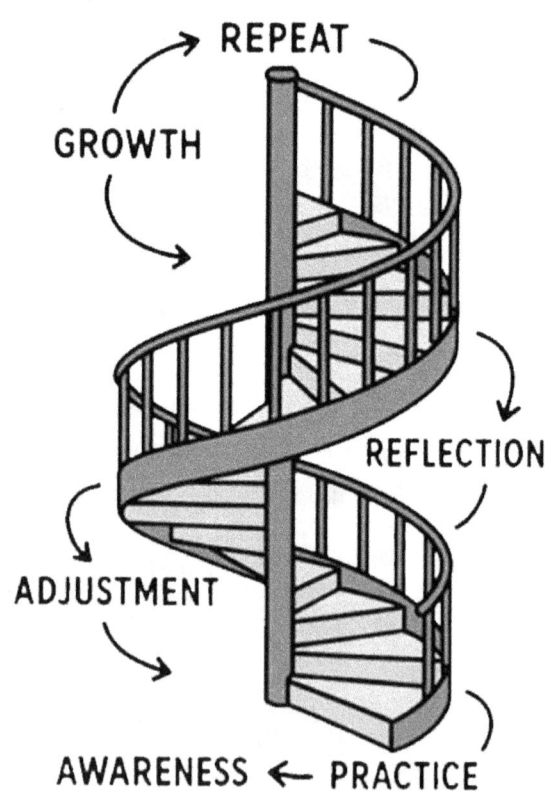

This spiral staircase graphic represents the continuous, upward journey of a lifelong learner. Each labeled step illustrates a vital phase in the cycle of personal and professional development:

1. **Awareness** – The journey begins with recognizing a need to learn or grow—whether it's a skill gap, a new concept, or a self-limiting mindset. Awareness is the spark that ignites curiosity and initiates growth.

2. **Practice** – Once aware, the learner takes action. Practice involves applying new knowledge or behaviors, testing ideas, and engaging in active learning experiences. It's the laboratory of learning.

3. **Reflection** – After practicing, the learner steps back to evaluate what worked, what didn't, and why. This introspection is key to transforming experiences into insight.

4. **Adjustment** – Insights from reflection lead to changes. Adjustments might include refining strategies, shifting mindsets, or setting new goals. This step is about flexibility and responsiveness.

5. **Growth** – As the learner adjusts and continues forward, real growth happens—competence increases, confidence builds, and new doors open.

6. **Repeat** – The staircase doesn't end. Each revolution of the spiral leads to higher levels of learning. Lifelong learners understand that mastery is not a destination but a journey of repeating this process continuously.

This visual metaphor encourages learners to embrace learning as an evolving, cyclical process—always climbing, always becoming.

The Lifelong Learner's Edge

The best leaders never stop learning. They read, reflect, adapt, and grow. But beneath their curiosity and discipline lies something deeper: **metacognition**—the engine that powers self-directed growth for a lifetime.

This chapter explores how metacognitive thinking transforms learning from a seasonal pursuit into a lifelong mission. Whether you're a teacher, coach, parent, pastor, or CEO, this kind of awareness can ignite resilience, adaptability, and wisdom at every stage of your leadership journey.

Cultivating a Metacognitive Mindset

To harness the power of metacognition as a catalyst for lifelong learning, individuals must cultivate a mindset that embraces reflection, adaptability, and self-awareness. This can be achieved through:

1. **Intentional Reflection**: Setting aside time for self-reflection allows learners to evaluate their experiences, identify strengths and weaknesses, and plan for future learning opportunities. For example, educators often encourage students to maintain reflective journals, fostering ongoing self-assessment that can lead to academic and personal growth.

2. **Embracing Curiosity**: A genuine desire to learn and explore new concepts fosters an environment where metacognition can thrive. By asking questions and seeking new experiences, individuals expand their knowledge and skills. Thomas Edison famously stated, "I have not failed.

Metacognition as a Catalyst for Lifelong Learning

I've just found 10,000 ways that won't work." This quote highlights the importance of curiosity and persistence in the learning process.

3. **Building a Supportive Community**: Surrounding oneself with like-minded individuals who value lifelong learning can enhance motivation and provide valuable insights. Learning communities, whether in-person or online, foster an environment of shared growth and exploration. For instance, platforms like Meetup facilitate connections among people with similar interests, creating opportunities for collaborative learning and exchange of ideas.

A Story of Lifelong Learning

There was a time early in my ministry when I was working with a young man named Jason, a volunteer who had been part of the church for a few years. Jason was talented—he could sing beautifully, play several instruments, and had a knack for leadership. But, despite all these gifts, he struggled to find his place. His energy was often misdirected, and his passion sometimes came across as impulsive or ungrounded.

One evening, after an especially challenging church service where tensions ran high, Jason approached me. His frustration was evident, and he questioned his role in the ministry. "I feel like I'm always trying hard, but nothing seems to stick," he admitted, the weight of self-doubt hanging heavy in his voice.

I didn't immediately offer advice or solutions. Instead, I asked Jason to reflect on his journey. "What's worked for you in the past? When have you felt most connected to God's work? What do you think might be missing now?" These questions weren't meant to provide immediate answers but to guide him through his own metacognitive process.

We spent the next hour discussing his past experiences—when he had felt most aligned with his purpose, what methods or strategies had helped him learn and grow, and where he had seen the most impact in his service. Through this conversation, Jason began to recognize that his struggles stemmed from trying to lead without reflecting on his personal strengths, needs, and learning processes. He had been so focused on external expectations that he had neglected the importance of understanding how he himself learned and grew.

Over the next few weeks, Jason started practicing metacognitive reflection. He took time to evaluate not just what he was doing but *how* he was doing it—how he was learning from each service, each challenge, and each victory. Slowly, he began to align his actions more closely with his strengths. He refined his leadership style, learned how to communicate more effectively with his team, and adopted strategies that played to his natural talents. Most importantly, he learned that failures were not setbacks but opportunities to refine his approach.

By the end of that year, Jason had not only become an integral part of the team but also a leader who inspired others to reflect on their own growth. His journey was a testament to the power of metacognition—not just in academic or professional contexts, but in the deepest aspects of our personal lives and spiritual growth. Reflecting on our journeys, adjusting our strategies, and learning from each step is what allows us to continue growing throughout our lives.

This story exemplifies how metacognition can transform struggles into stepping stones and enable us to learn from every experience. Jason's transformation didn't just come from external advice or quick fixes; it came from a willingness to pause, reflect, and intentionally adjust his approach—an essential practice for any lifelong learner.

What Makes Learning Stick?

We've all attended inspiring conferences or read powerful books, only to forget their lessons weeks later. Why?

Because **information doesn't equal transformation.**

Metacognition bridges the gap. It turns "I heard something interesting" into "I applied something meaningful." It allows leaders to:

- **Monitor how they learn**
- **Adapt strategies midstream**
- **Translate insight into habit**

It's the difference between consuming knowledge and cultivating growth.

Why Some Leaders Plateau

Plateaued leaders often:

- Stop asking questions
- Avoid feedback
- Stay in the comfort zone
- Delegate reflection instead of modeling it

Metacognitive leaders stay sharp because they:

- Embrace **learning as identity**
- Reflect **in motion**
- Admit what they don't know and pursue growth deliberately

Faith Integration – Proverbs 1:5

"Let the wise listen and add to their learning, and let the discerning get guidance."

Scripture invites us into a lifelong journey of wisdom—not a quick download of knowledge. True discipleship is fueled by reflection, correction, and application.

Ask God not just to reveal the truth, but to give you the insight to apply it. Ask for the discipline to continue learning when it's hard. That is the essence of a wise, metacognitive leader.

✓ Practical Applications

1. **Create a Weekly Learning Log** – Track new ideas you encounter and how you plan to apply them.
2. **Establish a Growth Habit** – Choose one consistent way to stretch your thinking (e.g., daily journaling, monthly book reflection, or peer coaching).
3. **Model Metacognitive Reflection** – As a leader, talk openly with your team about how you're learning, evolving, and making adjustments.
4. **Use "What Did I Learn Today?" As a Daily Reset** – Build this into your closing routine.

✓ Reflection and Renewal

God doesn't ask us to be perfect leaders—He asks us to be *teachable* ones.

Metacognition as a Catalyst for Lifelong Learning

Learning is a form of worship when it is done with a humble heart and a desire to grow in wisdom.

"Let the wise hear and increase in learning." —Proverbs 1:5

Lifelong learning, when fueled by metacognition, becomes spiritual formation in action.

✓ Reflection Questions

1. What consistent habits help me grow as a learner and leader?
2. Do I give myself time to reflect—or am I always rushing toward the next task?
3. What's one lesson I've recently learned that I haven't yet applied?

Team Activity – Lifelong Learner Mapping

Objective: Help your team reflect on and share their learning rhythms.

1. In small groups, ask team members to draw a simple map of their recent growth:

   - What new idea or habit have they adopted in the past month?
   - What has stretched their thinking most recently?

2. Have each person share one insight from the exercise.

3. As a team, identify how to support one another in sustaining learning habits.

Leadership Activity – The Learning Log

Step 1: Start a weekly "Learning Log."
Step 2: At the end of each week, write down:

- What you learned
- Where it came from (experience, reading, conversation)
- How you plan to apply it

Step 3: Revisit entries monthly to track your growth patterns.

This builds *ownership* of learning and turns passive exposure into active development.

✓ Final Thoughts

True leadership growth doesn't come from consuming more information—it comes from reflecting, applying, and evolving.

> **Metacognition turns life into a classroom, and every challenge into a teacher.**

Metacognition serves as a cornerstone for lifelong learning, empowering individuals to reflect on their experiences, adapt their strategies, and thrive in an ever-changing world. By cultivating a metacognitive mindset, we can lead ourselves and others toward a brighter future, filled with growth and understanding.

As Luke 6:45 reminds us, the treasures we cultivate within

ourselves shape our words and actions. By nurturing a heart filled with good through metacognitive awareness and a commitment to lifelong learning, we can make choices that lead to personal and communal transformation.

Lifelong learning isn't about collecting content. It's about cultivating wisdom.

The most effective, inspiring leaders are students first—of themselves, of others, of the world, and of God.

Reflect. Evolve. Lead. Then repeat.

Chapter 6

The Role of Leadership Development

"Effective leadership is not about making speeches or being liked; leadership is defined by results, not attributes."—Peter Drucker

As we navigate the intricacies of today's complex landscape, the role of effective leadership in fostering growth and innovation has never been more critical. Leadership development transcends traditional training methods; it encompasses a holistic approach that combines self-reflection, collaboration, and ongoing learning. This chapter delves into the importance of leadership development, drawing on real-life experiences from my journey as an educator, leader, writer, and pastor.

As a coach, I've had the privilege of mentoring young leaders. One such individual was a young pastor who struggled with balancing authority and compassion in his leadership. Through our time together, I encouraged him to reflect on his leadership decisions and think about how his emotions and assumptions influenced his actions. By developing the habit of reflective thinking, he began to see that his leadership style could evolve into one that was both firm and compassionate.

> *"The growth and development of people is the highest calling of leadership."*— Harvey S. Firestone

Leadership Is Not a Position—It's a Process

Great leadership is rarely born. It's built—day by day, reflection by reflection.

This chapter focuses on how leaders develop themselves and others through intentional structures, reflection, mentorship, and systems that support long-term growth. It's not enough to have great ideas—you must create a culture that multiplies growth.

Leadership development is how you build capacity for tomorrow, today.

Real-Life Example – Moses and Joshua

In Scripture, Moses didn't just lead—he developed a leader to follow him. Joshua wasn't selected by accident; he had been learning under Moses for years. He observed, served, asked questions, and made mistakes.

What stands out is Moses' **intentional mentoring**: He brought Joshua into sacred spaces, like the tent of meeting (Exodus 33:11), and gave him responsibility before handing over leadership.

Leaders don't leave legacies—they **develop legacies**.

Modern Example – Satya Nadella (CEO of Microsoft)

When Satya Nadella became CEO in 2014, Microsoft was losing its innovative edge. Rather than pushing new tech first, he focused on rebuilding the **leadership culture**—shifting from a know-it-all to a learn-it-all mindset.

The Role of Leadership Development

Nadella infused the company with a metacognitive culture:

- Promoting growth mindset
- Creating space for feedback loops
- Empowering others to learn from failure

The result? Microsoft's revival—and a generation of leaders who knew how to evolve.

Visual Framework – Leadership Development Cycle

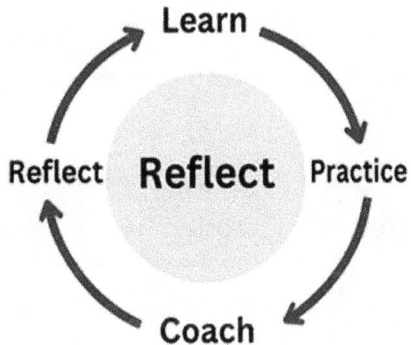

Leaders who evolve intentionally move through this loop constantly.

- **Reflect:** What kind of leader am I now?
- **Learn:** What do I need to grow?
- **Practice:** Where can I apply this now?
- **Coach:** Who else can I bring alongside me?
- **Multiply:** How can I reproduce growth in others?

Then the process restarts, stronger.

Personal Leadership Reflection – From Player to Coach to Multiplier

As a coach and campus leader, I began to see the difference between managing people and **developing leaders**. Managing stops at compliance. Development pushes toward capacity.

Early in my leadership, I focused heavily on direction and results. But over time, I saw that the most lasting change didn't come from directives—it came from investment. Sitting down with teachers. Listening. Reflecting with them. Challenging them to lead others.

One day, a teacher I'd mentored stepped into a leadership role and told me, "You didn't just give me permission to grow. You expected me to." That stayed with me.

True leadership development is expectation + relationship + reflection.

Biblical Foundation – 2 Timothy 2:2

> *"And the things you have heard me say . . . entrust to reliable people who will also be qualified to teach others."*

Paul didn't just build disciples—he built **leaders** who would build other leaders.

That's the multiplication mindset. And that's metacognitive leadership development.

Common Gaps in Leadership Growth

- **No reflection process** – leadership becomes routine
- **No coaching system** – people are promoted but not developed

- **No modeling of failure** – growth is stunted by fear
- **No cultural expectation** – leadership becomes accidental instead of intentional

Metacognition answers each of these. It makes leadership development **visible**, **repeatable**, and purpose-driven.

A Story of Transformational Leadership

One of the most profound moments in my career came during my time as a high school principal in a district facing a multitude of challenges. The school was grappling with low student engagement, dwindling morale among staff, and a sense of apathy that had permeated both the student body and the faculty. I knew that in order to change the culture, I had to begin by addressing the leadership within the school.

I called a meeting with my leadership team, where I shared my vision for transforming our school. I encouraged them not only to focus on improving test scores or disciplinary actions but to invest in building a culture of trust, engagement, and collaboration. It was not about one person having all the answers, but about empowering the entire team to be part of the solution.

Over the next few months, we rolled out several initiatives, but one of the most impactful was our new mentorship program. We paired struggling teachers with seasoned educators who could offer guidance and support. These relationships blossomed into powerful networks of growth. Teachers who had once been isolated in their classrooms began to share ideas, best practices, and strategies for improving student engagement.

The results were astounding. Not only did student engagement improve, but the school's culture shifted dramatically. Teachers felt supported, and students responded positively to the change in atmosphere. The key to this transformation was not my leadership alone; it was the collective efforts of a committed team that worked together toward a common goal. Leadership is about fostering that sense of shared responsibility and empowering others to take ownership of the change process.

The Need for Transformational Leadership

In my years of service in various educational roles, I have witnessed the impact of transformational leadership firsthand. A pivotal moment in my journey occurred during my tenure as an assistant principal in a struggling school. Faced with low morale among staff and students, I realized that effective leadership requires more than administrative skills; it necessitates the ability to inspire and empower others.

For example, I initiated regular "round-table" discussions where educators could voice their concerns, share successes, and collaborate on solutions. These meetings transformed the school culture, fostering a sense of community and shared purpose. By encouraging open dialogue, we not only identified challenges but also celebrated small victories, reinforcing the idea that leadership is about collective progress.

Cultivating a Growth Mindset

A key component of effective leadership development is cultivating a growth mindset among educators and leaders. This concept, popularized by psychologist Carol Dweck, emphasizes the belief that abilities and intelligence can be developed through dedication and hard work.

During my time as a pastor, I often shared this philosophy with my congregation, emphasizing that setbacks are not failures but opportunities for growth.

For instance, in a church leadership training session, I introduced a book study on *The 7 Habits of Highly Effective People* by Stephen Covey. Through discussions and reflections, we explored how effective habits can be applied in both spiritual and professional contexts.

Participants began to view challenges as learning experiences rather than insurmountable obstacles, fostering a culture of resilience that translated into their roles as educators.

Building Collaborative Networks

Effective leadership is not an isolated endeavor; it thrives in collaborative environments. Throughout my career, I have actively sought opportunities to connect with other educators and leaders. One memorable experience was co-hosting a professional development workshop with fellow administrators from neighboring districts.

We designed a series of sessions focused on instructional strategies that had proven successful in our schools. By sharing our experiences and resources, we created a rich learning environment where participants could gain insights from various perspectives. This collaborative effort not only enriched our professional practices but also built lasting relationships that continue to benefit our schools.

Embracing Continuous Learning

Leadership development is an ongoing journey that requires commitment to continuous learning. As an author, I often reflect on my experiences and share them through my writing, believing that storytelling can be a powerful tool for growth. In my book *The Meta-Cognitive Approach*, I emphasize the importance of self-awareness and reflection in effective leadership.

One significant moment that shaped my understanding of continuous learning was when I attended a leadership conference where I was exposed to innovative practices and emerging trends in education. Inspired by the ideas presented, I returned to my district determined to implement a mentorship program pairing experienced educators with new teachers. This initiative fostered professional growth for both mentors and mentees, illustrating how a commitment to learning can create a ripple effect throughout the educational community.

✓ Practical Applications

1. **Identify a Leadership Pipeline** – Map out who you're mentoring and how you're intentionally developing them.

2. **Create a Leadership Reflection Template** – Help leaders track goals, reflect weekly, and journal their development journey.

3. **Model Vulnerability and Growth** – Share openly about your leadership evolution to encourage others to grow with confidence.

4. **Implement Leadership Check-Ins** – Hold brief monthly one-on-ones focused only on reflection and development, not performance.

✓ Reflection and Renewal

Jesus didn't just teach the crowds—He developed twelve individuals deeply and intentionally. He equipped them, challenged them, and then released them to lead.

> *"And the things you have heard me say . . . entrust to reliable people who will also be qualified to teach others."* —2 Timothy 2:2

Your calling as a leader is not just to grow, but to **multiply growth** in others. Leadership development is a spiritual mandate, not just an organizational goal.

✓ Final Thoughts

Developing leaders is one of the most powerful investments you will ever make. But it doesn't happen by accident.

It happens through reflection, intentionality, and modeling the kind of leadership you hope to multiply.

The journey of leadership development is essential for cultivating effective educators and fostering a vibrant learning environment. By prioritizing self-reflection, embracing collaboration, and committing to continuous growth, we can redefine what it means to lead in education.

As Peter Drucker reminds us, true leadership is defined by results. When we invest in our growth as leaders, we not only enhance our capabilities but also empower those around us to thrive. Through intentional leadership development, we can inspire a new generation of educators and leaders who are equipped to navigate the complexities of education and transform the lives of their students. Let us embrace this calling, guided by a commitment to lifelong learning and a passion for inspiring others on their educational journeys.

✓ Reflection Questions

1. Who are you currently developing—and how?
2. What part of your leadership journey has been most formative?
3. What structure or rhythm do you have in place for long-term leadership growth?

✓ Team Activity – Leadership Web Mapping

Objective: Visualize your team's leadership growth and identify gaps.

1. On a whiteboard or digital canvas, write your name in the center.
2. Draw lines to the people you've mentored or directly developed.
3. Ask each of them to do the same, mapping who they've helped grow.
4. Review the map as a team. Identify:
    - Where growth is thriving
    - Where leadership development is missing
    - Who needs to be equipped next

Reflection Prompts

1. Who has invested in your leadership development—and how?
2. Who are you currently developing? Are they aware of it?
3. What structure do you have for reflecting on your growth as a leader?

Closing Thought

Leaders aren't just born. They're built—by leaders who reflect, invest, challenge, and evolve. Build the systems. Build the people. Then step back and watch how many others begin to rise.

Reflect. Equip. Multiply.

Chapter 7

Promoting Self-Regulated Learning

"Discipline is the bridge between goals and accomplishment."
—Jim Rohn

In our rapidly changing world, the ability to learn autonomously and effectively has never been more important. Self-regulated learning (SRL) empowers individuals to take charge of their educational processes, fostering independence and adaptability. This chapter explores the concept of self-regulated learning, its significance in education, and how we can cultivate these essential skills as educators, leaders, and mentors.

What Is Self-Regulated Learning?

Self-regulated learning (SRL) is the ability to guide your own learning through planning, monitoring, reflection, and adjustment. In leadership, SRL translates into **intentional growth**—the ability to stay focused, reflect midstream, and adapt wisely.

In my years of teaching, one of the most powerful moments came when a student began to take ownership of her learning. At first, she struggled with time management, but after I guided her to reflect on her learning habits and goals, she began to improve. The power of self-regulation came when she realized that her success was directly tied to her ability to reflect on her progress and adjust her strategies.

John Maxwell's teachings align with this process, emphasizing the importance of personal responsibility in leadership. He often talks about how successful leaders take ownership of their actions and learn from their experiences. By encouraging others to reflect on their learning and set goals, we empower them to become more self-regulated, leading to greater success.

The 3 Phases of Self-Regulated Learning

1. **Forethought:** Goal-setting, planning, anticipating challenges
2. **Performance:** Monitoring, focus, using strategies, managing emotions
3. **Reflection:** Evaluating outcomes, adjusting effort or methods

Real-Life Example – Angela Duckworth & Grit

Angela Duckworth's research on grit shows that long-term success often has less to do with talent and more to do with **self-regulation**: persistence, passion, and purpose over time.

Gritty individuals don't just work harder—they monitor and adapt. They reflect. They keep going because their learning is not externally motivated—it's self-driven.

Leadership Example – U.S. Navy SEALs

One of the most powerful examples of SRL in action comes from Navy SEAL training. Recruits are taught not just physical discipline but **mental resilience.**

They reflect constantly under stress:

- What's working?
- What needs to change?
- How can I push through this moment wisely?

The leaders who emerge from this training don't just react. They adapt with composure and clarity.

Personal Reflection

In my years as a coach, I began noticing that the best athletes weren't always the most talented. They were the ones who could **adjust in real time**—who didn't wait for the coach to fix things.

That's when I started teaching players to self-correct. I'd ask them:

- What are you seeing?
- What's your plan for next time?

Those conversations changed the culture of our team. It wasn't just about executing the game plan—it was about becoming a learner on the field. That's SRL in motion. That's leadership from the inside out.

Faith Integration – 1 Corinthians 9:27

"But I discipline my body and keep it under control, lest after preaching to others I myself should be disqualified."

The Apostle Paul reminds us that self-regulation is both spiritual and practical. To lead others, we must first **lead ourselves**—with discipline, reflection, and grace.

A Powerful Story of Transformation

When I think of self-regulated learning, I am reminded of one student who completely transformed her academic journey through the power of reflection and perseverance. Her name was Emily, and at the start of the school year, she struggled with motivation and organization. She often found herself overwhelmed by assignments, unable to prioritize her tasks, and frequently missed deadlines. As her teacher, I noticed her growing frustration, but I also saw something else: a deep desire to succeed, though she lacked the strategies to get there.

One day after class, I asked Emily to stay behind. I could see the weight of her struggles in her eyes, but I also knew that she had untapped potential. I guided her through a simple exercise: I asked her to reflect on what was working in her study habits and what wasn't. We then set small, manageable goals together, and I encouraged her to monitor her progress, adjusting her strategies as needed.

Over the next few months, something remarkable began to happen. Emily started organizing her tasks, breaking them into smaller chunks, and using a planner to track her progress. Each week, we reviewed her goals and reflected on her achievements, no matter how small. She began to realize that her success was directly tied to her ability to take ownership of her learning.

Promoting Self-Regulated Learning

One day, Emily came to me with a smile that I will never forget. She had aced a major exam, something she had never believed was possible for her. It wasn't just the grade that made her proud; it was the realization that through self-regulation—setting goals, monitoring her progress, and reflecting on her learning—she had transformed her academic approach. She was no longer at the mercy of her circumstances but was in control of her own learning journey.

Emily's story is a testament to the power of self-regulated learning. By guiding her to reflect, set goals, and take ownership, we unlocked the potential for her success. This is the essence of self-regulation: it's not just about managing time or completing tasks, but about taking responsibility for one's own growth, overcoming obstacles, and adapting to challenges. This process is a critical life skill that transcends the classroom, shaping individuals into resilient and autonomous learners.

Self-regulated learning is the foundation of lifelong growth. It encourages learners to become actively engaged in their educational journeys by taking ownership of their goals, progress, and outcomes. In my experience, self-regulated learning is not just about managing time or completing tasks—it is about cultivating a mindset of responsibility, resilience, and self-awareness. Like Emily, students and individuals can learn to assess their progress, reflect on what strategies work for them, and adjust their approach when necessary. By developing these skills, they are better equipped to navigate challenges and find success, both in the classroom and beyond.

This process of self-regulation is a dynamic one, involving a blend of cognitive, metacognitive, and behavioral skills. It requires learners to set goals, monitor their progress, reflect on their strategies, and, ultimately, take control of their own learning journey. When these skills are cultivated, individuals become more independent, adaptable, and capable of thriving in an ever-changing world.

The story of Emily encapsulates the core principles of self-regulated learning, and as we explore these concepts further in this chapter, I hope it inspires you to think about how you can encourage self-regulation in those you lead, teach, and mentor.

Through goal setting, self-monitoring, reflection, and persistence, we empower others to become lifelong learners—just as Emily did. Let's dive deeper into these components of SRL and how we can foster them in the learners we serve.

Understanding Self-Regulated Learning

Self-regulated learning is a dynamic process through which learners set goals, monitor their progress, and reflect on their learning strategies and outcomes. It involves a blend of cognitive, metacognitive, and behavioral skills that enable individuals to own their educational journeys. Key components of SRL include:

- **Goal Setting:** Effective learners identify specific, achievable goals that guide their efforts. I remember coaching a high school football team where we encouraged each player to set personal performance goals for the season. One player aimed to improve his passing accuracy. By breaking it down into smaller weekly targets—like practicing throws during off-hours—he not only improved his skills but also became more confident on the field.

- **Self-Monitoring:** This involves tracking one's understanding and performance, enabling learners to adjust strategies as needed. As a pastor, I encourage my congregation to reflect on their spiritual journeys. In one Bible study, I introduced the practice of weekly self-assessment where participants would note their spiritual growth, challenges, and areas for improvement. This simple act of reflection led to deeper discussions and personal revelations.

- **Self-Reflection:** Reflecting on learning experiences helps individuals evaluate their effectiveness. During my teaching years, I had my students keep reflection journals. After each major project, they would write about what strategies worked, what didn't, and how they felt about their learning. This practice cultivated a culture of introspection that empowered them to take control of their learning.

- **Motivation and Persistence:** Self-regulated learners remain motivated and resilient, understanding that setbacks are part of the process. I recall a moment in my teaching career when a student faced multiple rejections from college applications. Instead of giving up, we reframed the situation as a learning opportunity, discussing what could be improved for the next round of applications. His perseverance and self-reflection eventually led him to a university that was a perfect fit for him.

The Importance of Self-Regulated Learning

Self-regulated learning is essential in education for several reasons:

- **Fostering Lifelong Learning:** SRL skills prepare individuals to become lifelong learners. A graduate from a local community college once shared how the self-regulated learning strategies he developed helped him adapt to new challenges in his career, allowing him to upskill effectively in a rapidly evolving job market.

- **Enhancing Academic Achievement:** Research consistently shows that self-regulated learners achieve higher academic performance because they take initiative and seek help when needed. In my experience as a school leader, I witnessed this firsthand when we implemented a student-led conference model. Students who prepared for and led their conferences showed remarkable improvements in ownership of their learning and academic success.

- **Encouraging Critical Thinking:** SRL promotes critical thinking as learners engage in self-reflection. In a graduate seminar I facilitated, students were required to critically evaluate their arguments and engage in peer discussions. This led to richer dialogue and deeper understanding, transforming how they approached complex topics.

- **Building Confidence:** Taking control of their learning helps individuals develop confidence in their abilities. As I often tell my students and congregants, "The only limit to your impact is your imagination and commitment." Encouraging them to regulate their own learning empowers them to realize their potential.

Cultivating a Self-Regulated Learning Mindset

While various tools and resources can enhance self-regulated learning, cultivating a mindset that values and promotes these skills is crucial. Here's how we can encourage SRL:

- **Modeling Self-Regulation:** As leaders, we must demonstrate our self-regulated learning practices. In my role as a principal, I shared my experiences of pursuing professional development. By openly discussing the challenges I faced and how I overcame them, I inspired my staff to embrace similar practices in their own growth.

- **Encouraging Goal Setting:** Providing opportunities for students and team members to set their own goals fosters ownership and accountability. During a leadership retreat, I guided attendees through creating SMART goals for their personal and professional lives. This exercise not only increased engagement but also established a culture of goal-oriented growth.

- **Promoting Reflection:** Creating a culture of reflection encourages individuals to evaluate their learning processes. In my church, we often hold reflection sessions where members share their personal growth stories, challenges, and successes. This practice deepens their understanding and commitment to their faith and personal development.

- **Providing Support and Resources:** Ensure that individuals have access to the tools and resources they need for self-regulated learning. During my time in education, I introduced various online platforms that offered personalized learning experiences. These resources, when coupled with guidance, enabled students to pursue their learning pathways confidently.

Self-regulated learning is an essential skill in today's educational landscape, empowering individuals to take charge of their journeys. By fostering independence, critical thinking, and resilience, SRL prepares learners to thrive in an ever-evolving world.

As Romans 12:2 reminds us, transformation begins with the renewal of our minds. By embracing self-regulated learning, we can cultivate a generation of learners who are adaptable, reflective, and empowered to discern what is good and acceptable in their pursuit of knowledge.

In this journey of promoting self-regulated learning, we find a powerful pathway to enhance educational experiences, creating a future where learners are equipped to navigate challenges, embrace opportunities, and lead lives of purpose and significance. Together, let us reflect, evolve, and lead, fostering environments that empower everyone to become self-regulated learners.

The SRL Cycle

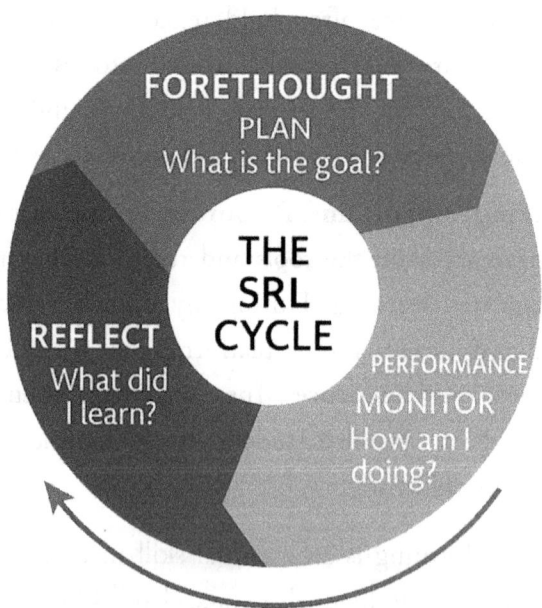

- **Plan:** What is the goal?
- **Monitor:** How am I doing?

- **Reflect:** What did I learn?
- **Adjust:** What will I do next time?

This is not a loop of perfection—but of progress.

How Leaders Promote SRL in Others

1. **Model It:** Talk about your own learning and thinking openly.
2. **Make It Visible:** Use tools like goal logs, reflection journals, or weekly recaps.
3. **Encourage Self-Talk:** "What's my next step?" "What went wrong—and why?"
4. **Coach, Don't Control:** Let others fail forward and support their evaluation process.
5. **Celebrate Growth, Not Just Results.**

Reflection Questions

1. Do I make time to reflect on my own leadership process—or just the outcomes?
2. Do I model self-regulated learning publicly with my team?
3. What system do I have in place to adjust my goals and strategies regularly?

Team Activity – SRL Check-In Routine

Each week, invite your team or students to answer these questions:

- What was your goal this week?
- What helped or hindered your success?
- What's one adjustment you'll make for next week?

Build the habit. It creates ownership and accountability.

From Compliance to Ownership

True leadership doesn't stop at directing others—it builds their capacity to lead themselves. Promoting self-regulated learning (SRL) in others means creating an environment where people take ownership of their growth, think critically, and reflect consistently.

You, as a leader, can coach, model, and release responsibility in a way that builds self-driven thinkers—whether you're leading students, teachers, staff, or your own children.

What Does SRL Look Like in Others?

When someone is self-regulated, they:

- Set meaningful goals
- Monitor their progress
- Adapt strategies when challenges arise
- Reflect honestly on results
- Stay intrinsically motivated

Your role isn't to micromanage those behaviors—it's to create the conditions in which they can thrive.

Real-Life Example – Anne Sullivan and Helen Keller

Anne Sullivan's work with Helen Keller is a powerful model of promoting SRL. At first, Sullivan provided full guidance, but as Keller learned, Sullivan gradually stepped back—allowing Helen to own her process.

What made Sullivan remarkable wasn't just her teaching—it was her belief that Helen could think, reflect, and grow. She gave Keller space to fail and tools to reflect. That belief empowered one of the greatest minds of her generation to emerge from silence.

Personal Reflection – Shifting from Control to Coaching

In my early leadership years, I often felt the pressure to make sure everything went right. That meant holding tight to decisions, fixing problems myself, and walking others through every step. But over time, I realized I wasn't building confident, self-driven people—I was building dependence. So I shifted.

I started coaching with questions:

- What do you think should happen next?
- How would you handle this if I weren't here?
- What did you learn from that moment?

And something incredible happened. People stopped waiting for permission—and started growing.

Biblical Example – Jesus and the Disciples

Jesus spent years modeling faith, wisdom, and service. But He didn't keep His disciples in passive learning forever. He sent them out—first in pairs, then later to the nations.

He empowered them to reflect, to rely on the Spirit, and to grow through action. That's what leaders do—they release responsibility when the time is right.

Visual Framework – Gradual Release of Responsibility

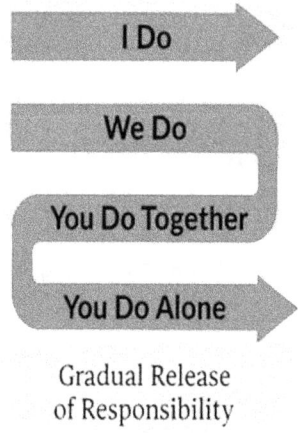

Gradual Release of Responsibility

This instructional model applies to leadership, too:

- I Do: Model metacognition and reflection out loud.
- We Do: Collaborate in planning, problem-solving, and adjusting.
- You Do Together: Encourage peer accountability and shared leadership.

- You Do Alone: Step back. Let others lead, reflect, and own outcomes.

Culture Builders That Promote SRL

- Ask before advising. Teach people to reflect before you jump in.
- Celebrate self-awareness. "You noticed that—great metacognition."
- Normalize failure and feedback. Let growth be messy.
- Create routines for goal-setting, check-ins, and reflection.
- Give clear frameworks—but freedom within them.

Real-Life Example – Booker T. Washington

Washington, founder of Tuskegee Institute, believed in the dignity of self-reliance. He trained students not just with knowledge, but with habits of self-discipline, delayed gratification, and reflective improvement.

He once said, "Success is to be measured not so much by the position that one has reached in life as by the obstacles which he has overcome while trying to succeed."

Washington promoted SRL before it had a name. He believed that building capacity in people required trust, guidance, and release.

Reflection Prompts

1. Am I doing too much for those I lead?

2. How do I respond when someone struggles—do I coach, or do I take over?
3. What structure do I have in place to support goal-setting, monitoring, and reflection?

Team Activity – Release Map

Think of a skill or responsibility your team needs to own. Together, map out:

- What *you* will model
- What *you and they* will do together
- When *they* will take the lead
- How you'll debrief the process

Use this framework to develop leaders in every layer of your team.

Leadership isn't control—it's cultivation.

The greatest gift you can give those you lead is the confidence, space, and structure to grow themselves.

Closing Thought

Self-regulated leaders don't wait to be told how to grow—they take initiative. They reflect mid-race. They evolve, even when it's uncomfortable.

Lead from the inside out. Teach others to do the same.

Reflect. Regulate. Lead. Repeat.

Chapter 8

"Evolve" as a Tool for Metacognition

"And do not be conformed to this world, but be transformed by the renewing of your mind, so that you may prove what the will of God is, that which is good and acceptable and perfect."— Romans 12:2 (NASB)

The journey of growth described in Romans is one of continual renewal and transformation, a truth that resonates deeply with educators and leaders in today's fast-paced educational landscape. The concept of "Evolve" serves as a powerful metaphor for this growth, encouraging us to adapt, learn, and enhance our practices through reflective metacognition. By incorporating metacognitive tools like "Evolve," we not only refine our skills but also strengthen our capacity to inspire positive change within our schools and communities.

Metacognition is not just about understanding where we are; it's about knowing where we're going. I've had several counseling sessions where individuals were stuck in self-limiting beliefs, unable to see their potential. One such case involved a young man who was convinced he would never succeed in leadership. After I guided him through a process of reflection, he began to evolve. He recognized that his beliefs about his limitations were rooted in past failures, not in his actual potential.

What Does It Mean to Evolve?

To evolve means to:

- Adjust when reality shifts
- Reassess what's working and what's not
- Stay aligned with purpose while changing methods
- Learn from feedback, failure, and faith

Leaders who evolve don't just **change**—they **grow forward** with wisdom.

Practical Applications of Evolve in Leadership

1. Goal Setting Through Reflection and Metacognition

Ask:

- What needs to change in my current leadership approach?
- What feedback have I received that I haven't fully processed?

Example: As a principal, I once led PD sessions that fell flat. After reflecting using the "Evolve" mindset, I redesigned them with input from staff. The change led to improved engagement and outcomes. Reflection turned failure into refinement.

2. Transforming Challenges into Growth Opportunities

Scripture reminds us to *"count it all joy when you encounter various trials"* (James 1:2-4). Every challenge is a classroom for growth.

Example: A new curriculum once overwhelmed our district. Initial frustration turned into collaborative innovation as we chose to evolve rather than resist. Reflecting on our shared struggles unified our teams.

3. Building a Culture of Reflective Collaboration

Evolving isn't a solo act. It's communal.

Example: I initiated "reflective circles" in team meetings. We asked: What worked? What didn't? What can we try next? This practice birthed a culture of ownership and accountability.

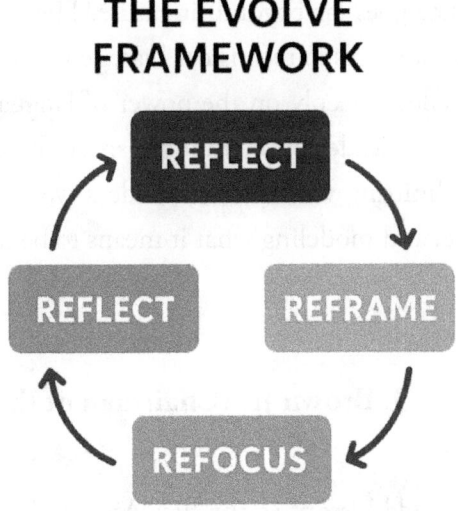

Leaders Who Embodied Evolution of the Mind

Dr. Vivek Murthy (U.S. Surgeon General)

As the nation's doctor, Dr. Murthy has consistently emphasized the emotional and mental well-being of individuals and communities. What makes his leadership remarkable is his openness about loneliness, burnout, and the human need for connection—even among high achievers. His willingness to reflect on public health not just through data but through empathy and self-awareness shows how leaders must evolve with the needs of the people they serve. He models vulnerability and courage in the face of systemic challenges.

Chimamanda Ngozi Adichie (Author and Cultural Commentator)

Adichie's influence goes far beyond literature. Her talks and writings challenge global audiences to reconsider bias, gender roles, and cultural narratives. She reflects deeply on the power of language and perspective. Her growth as a leader in the thought space comes from her ability to evolve—admitting when her early ideas were limited, growing through dialogue, and modeling what it means to be intellectually and socially agile.

General Charles Q. Brown Jr. (Chairman of the Joint Chiefs of Staff)

General Brown made history as the first African American to lead a U.S. military service branch. He is known for his transparent leadership, especially after the death of George Floyd, when he released a powerful video sharing his experiences with racism in the military.

His message was not only reflective, it was transformative. He challenged an entire institution to evolve. His career reflects a metacognitive leader—assessing, adjusting, and aligning his leadership to create greater equity and purpose.

How Leaders "Evolve" in Practice

1. **Using Reflection to Reframe Challenges**

    A superintendent facing low teacher morale might begin by asking hard questions: "What systems or messages have contributed to this culture?" By gathering feedback, revisiting communication practices, and making room for teacher voice, the leader reframes the challenge not as a burden but as an opportunity to evolve in communication and culture-building.

2. **Learning Publicly**

    Leaders who evolve are not afraid to admit mistakes or gaps in knowledge. A campus principal who receives negative feedback on a failed initiative might share openly at a staff meeting: "Here's what I learned . . . Here's what I'll do differently." This public processing builds trust and models reflective leadership.

3. **Aligning Vision with Behavior**

    Evolving means not just saying the right things but behaving consistently with core values. A leader cannot claim to value collaboration yet lead in isolation. Self-checks, journaling, coaching, and peer accountability can help keep alignment in focus.

Supporting the Evolve Process with AI

Modern tools—including AI—can accelerate metacognitive growth for today's leaders:

- **Real-Time Feedback**: AI platforms can analyze school culture survey data or classroom walkthrough trends, alerting leaders to disconnects between vision and reality.
- **Reflection Prompts**: AI-driven coaching apps can prompt daily or weekly questions that guide leadership self-reflection (e.g., "What went well this week? What do you wish you had done differently?").
- **Scenario Simulation**: Some platforms offer simulated decision-making situations, allowing leaders to practice ethical or strategic judgment and receive tailored feedback.
- **Time and Task Audits**: Leaders can use AI tools to audit how they spend time, revealing whether they are investing in people, visibility, and key priorities, or being consumed by operational noise.

Faith-Focused Application: A Leader Transformed

In my own journey, I (Dr. Teddy Ott) recall a time when I was overwhelmed by responsibility as both an educational leader and a pastor. I was reactive, often responding out of pressure instead of clarity. But through prayer and intentional reflection, I began setting boundaries, delegating effectively, and renewing my focus on God's calling—not people's expectations. That process—rooted in Scripture and metacognitive awareness—allowed me to evolve. I wasn't just doing more; I was leading better.

"Growth is painful. Change is painful. But nothing is as painful as staying stuck somewhere you don't belong."— Mandy Hale

Evolving is not about perfection—it's about progress. It is a sacred act to pause, assess, repent when needed, and press on with renewed purpose. For today's educators and leaders, evolution is not optional. The students we serve, the staff we lead, and the futures we shape demand nothing less.

Let *Evolve* be more than a chapter—it should be your lifestyle.

Embracing "Evolve" for Lifelong Growth

The concept of "Evolve" empowers educators to cultivate a mindset of adaptability, resilience, and continuous growth. By combining metacognitive practices with the insights offered by AI-driven coaching, we can refine our approaches and enhance our impact within our educational communities. Embracing "Evolve" aligns with the biblical call to renewal and transformation, urging us to grow in wisdom, understanding, and purpose.

As we integrate "Evolve" into our educational leadership, we pave the way for a generation of educators who are resilient, reflective, and empowered to create meaningful change. By prioritizing continuous growth and adapting to new insights, we lead by example, inspiring our students to develop the same commitment to lifelong learning and improvement.

A Personal Journey of Evolution

As I reflect on my own journey as a leader, I am reminded of how deeply the process of evolution—both in mindset and in practice—has shaped my work. Early in my career, I believed leadership was about having the answers, knowing all the right things, and being the one to provide solutions. However, as I gained experience, I came to realize that leadership is far more about listening, reflecting, and learning. The most profound shifts in my leadership came not from external changes but from internal ones: changes in my thinking, my approach to challenges, and my interactions with others.

There were moments of failure that taught me more than any success could. I remember a specific instance early in my tenure as a principal when I faced resistance from a faculty member who was particularly difficult to work with. I initially tried to "fix" the situation by asserting authority, but it quickly became apparent that this approach wasn't effective. It wasn't until I took the time to reflect on my own actions and motivations that I recognized my own need to evolve. I realized that leadership wasn't just about managing people—it was about inspiring them, engaging them in their own growth, and meeting them where they were. This shift in perspective not only transformed my relationship with that faculty member but also influenced how I led my entire team moving forward.

Over time, I began to adopt more reflective practices in all aspects of my leadership, from setting goals to navigating challenges. I learned that by continually evolving my thinking, I could foster a culture of growth, trust, and collaboration within my school. Every challenge became an opportunity to refine my methods, better understand my staff, and align our efforts with the broader vision we shared.

Now, I view leadership as a journey of constant self-reflection and evolution. Even today, as I take on new roles and face new challenges, I continue to reflect on my practices, question my assumptions, and adjust my approach. I recognize that leadership is not a static role—it's one of perpetual growth. I am committed to evolving as a leader and, in doing so, to inspiring others to do the same.

The Power of Evolution in Leadership

Great leaders don't just reflect—they **evolve**. They change strategically, driven by insight and anchored in purpose.

Metacognition empowers leaders to evolve with clarity: not reacting to every shift in the wind, but adapting thoughtfully to what matters most.

This chapter explores how personal and organizational evolution, when rooted in reflection, becomes a powerful leadership tool.

My Personal Leadership Journey – From Intentions to Impact

For years, I was known for my energy, clarity, and direction. But over time, I noticed something unsettling: I was still pushing forward, but people around me felt behind. I realized I had built momentum—but not movement.

That realization hurt. But it also invited me into one of the most transformational shifts in my leadership life.

I began evolving—less driven by outcomes, more by insight. I began asking:

- What's missing in the system I've built?
- Am I empowering or just managing?
- What does excellence look like—beyond compliance?

That evolution changed how I coach, lead, and reflect. It didn't start with a strategy. It started with a mirror.

Faith Integration – Seasons of Refinement

Ecclesiastes 3 reminds us that *"to everything there is a season."* Leadership has seasons too:

- Seasons to build
- Seasons to break and reassess
- Seasons to pivot and begin again

God often uses discomfort as a **refining fire**, shaping us into who we need to become.

> **Evolution in leadership is not abandoning identity—
> it's deepening it.**

Real-Life Example – Howard Schultz (Starbucks)

Schultz stepped down from Starbucks, only to return years later when the brand lost focus. His evolution as a leader was not about ego but about values.

He re-centered the company on its core mission: human connection. He simplified product lines, reinvested in employee experience, and brought reflection into corporate culture.

He evolved—not just to save the business, but to revive its soul.

The Evolve Cycle – A Metacognitive Framework

- **Reflect:** What is working? What isn't?
- **Adapt:** What needs to shift—strategy, mindset, method?
- **Act:** Apply the change purposefully.

- **Refine:** Adjust based on feedback, observation, and prayer.
- **Repeat:** Growth is not linear—it's cyclical.

This cycle ensures that change is not reactive but **responsive** and mission-aligned.

Signs a Leader Needs to Evolve

- Fatigue with the familiar
- Stalled progress despite effort
- Feedback that feels repetitive
- Frustration in high-capacity teams
- A sense that you're leading from memory, not from presence

These are not failures—they're **invitations to evolve**.

Team Reflection Exercise – The Evolve Audit

Invite your leadership team to reflect on:

- What's not working that we keep pretending *is*?
- What process or system needs to be reimagined?
- Who on the team needs more voice, space, or support to grow?

Use their insights to fuel purposeful change.

Closing Thought

Evolving doesn't mean abandoning what's sacred—it means honoring it enough to keep improving.

Leadership is a journey of *Reflecting. Adapting. Acting. Refining. Repeating.*

That's how you build a life—and a legacy—that grows deeper, not just wider.

Chapter 9

Case Studies and Research: Metacognition and Impact on Learning Outcomes

"Learning without reflection is a waste. Reflection without learning is dangerous."— Confucius

Why Case Studies Matter

It's one thing to believe in metacognition. It's another to see it **in action**—transforming learning, leadership, and life. This chapter brings together powerful stories, research evidence, and real-world applications that show exactly how reflective thinking changes outcomes.

As we delve into the profound connection between metacognition and effective educational practices, it's essential to explore real-world examples and case studies that highlight how these concepts significantly impact learning outcomes. By analyzing various applications, we can glean insights into how metacognitive practices can enhance educational experiences and student success, particularly in the context of standardized assessments and accountability measures.

As a leader in education, I've seen firsthand the impact of metacognition on student outcomes. One case study I recall involved a group of struggling students who were encouraged to engage in reflective journaling. Over time, students who practiced self-reflection showed significant improvement not only in their academic performance but in their confidence and self-awareness.

This is consistent with John Maxwell's assertion that leadership is about helping others grow. By creating environments where individuals are encouraged to reflect on their actions and decisions, we create opportunities for growth and improvement. The impact of metacognitive strategies is measurable, and they lead to both personal and academic success.

The Importance of Metacognition in Learning

Metacognition—the awareness and regulation of one's own thinking processes—has been consistently linked to improved academic performance and deeper learning. Throughout my career, I have seen how students who engage in metacognitive practices are more equipped to set goals, monitor their progress, and reflect on their learning strategies. This ultimately leads to a greater understanding and retention of knowledge.

For instance, during my tenure as a principal in Texas, we initiated a program where students participated in regular reflection sessions after significant assessments. We encouraged them to ask themselves, "What strategies worked best for me?" and "How can I approach the next test differently?" The outcomes were significant: Students began taking ownership of their learning, resulting in a noticeable improvement in their test scores.

Leadership Reflection – The Shift Is Worth It

I've seen metacognition transform entire teams. Once people start thinking about their thinking—individually and together—it changes culture. You move from defense to ownership. From blame to adjustment. From static leadership to evolving influence.

Faith Integration – "Be Doers of the Word . . ." (James 1:22)

Scripture reminds us that reflection must lead to action. *"Be doers of the word, and not hearers only, deceiving yourselves."*

Metacognitive leadership asks:

- What is God teaching me?
- What have I done with it?
- What will I do next?

Reflection Prompts

- What systems do I have in place that encourage reflective growth?
- How can I model metacognition more visibly to my team or students?
- What's one practice from these case studies I could implement next week?

Closing Thought

The data is in. The stories are real. And the impact is lasting.

Metacognition isn't just a strategy—it's a shift in how we lead, learn, and live.

Reflect. Study. Grow. Then do it again.

Case Study #1 – Metacognitive Journals in a Middle School Classroom

A Texas middle school implemented **weekly reflection journals** in their 7th-grade science class. Students wrote about what they understood, where they struggled, and how they could adjust their strategies.

In just one semester:

- Test scores rose 14%
- Students began using self-talk strategies
- Classroom behavior improved due to increased self-awareness

The metacognitive strategy didn't just help them **learn science**—
it helped them learn how to **learn.**

Case Study #2 – Coaching Conversations in a Rural School

In a small district under my leadership, leadership coaching was redesigned to focus on **metacognitive reflection**. After teacher observations, leaders no longer just gave feedback—they asked reflective questions:

Metacognition and Impact on Learning Outcomes

- What led you to that instructional decision?
- What would you do differently tomorrow?
- What did you notice about student responses?

Over the next 18 months:

- Teacher retention increased
- Trust between staff and leaders grew
- Teachers began coaching each other organically

We stopped chasing compliance and started cultivating capacity.

Case Study #3 – A Church's Shift to Reflective Discipleship

A local church transitioned its small group structure from lecture-based to **question-based reflection**. Groups now center around:

- What is God showing me through this passage?
- How am I responding to conviction or encouragement?
- Where do I need to grow this week?

As a result, group engagement deepened. Members reported:

- Greater spiritual maturity
- Increased personal accountability
- Higher attendance and involvement

*Reflection led to **transformation.***

Key Research Findings

- **Zimmerman (2002):** Self-regulated learners outperform peers academically because they reflect, plan, and monitor their learning more intentionally.
- **Hattie & Donoghue (2016):** Metacognitive strategies rank among the **top 10 influences on student achievement** in a synthesis of 1,200 meta-analyses.
- **Duckworth (2013):** Grit—tied closely to self-regulation—is more predictive of success than IQ.

In other words, metacognition isn't fluff—it's a proven factor in long-term success.

Visual – Comparison Infographic

TRADITIONAL LEARNING versus METACOGNITION

TRADITIONAL LEARNING	METACOGNITION
What to learn	How to learn
How to learn	Awareness of thinking process
Practicing	Strategic practicing

Aspect	Traditional Approach	Metacognitive Approach
Motivation	External (grades, rewards)	Internal (goals, purpose)
Error Response	Avoid or ignore	Analyze and learn
Strategy Use	Passive repetition	Intentional adaptation
Self-Talk	Rare or negative	Frequent and empowering
Performance	Inconsistent	Continually improving

The Power of Reflection in Overcoming Adversity

I recall a particularly poignant story from my time as a leader that underscores the deep connection between reflection and overcoming challenges. It involved a group of senior high students who were faced with an advanced algebra exam. The students had struggled with the subject throughout the semester, and their anxieties about the exam were palpable. One student, in particular, stood out—Chris, a bright but often disengaged student, who had consistently struggled with both his grades and his confidence in mathematics.

As part of a larger initiative to incorporate metacognitive practices across subjects, we began a week of reflective journaling just before the final exam. Students were encouraged to journal not only about their preparation and study habits but also about how they felt about the upcoming test and what past challenges had taught them about their learning style. The focus was on understanding the process rather than just the outcome.

Chris, initially skeptical about the process, wrote in his journal, "I always feel like I don't know what I'm doing when I get to the test. I freeze and can't remember the things I've studied. But maybe if I think about how I've solved problems before, I might have a better shot." This simple reflection became a turning point for him. Over the next few days, he consciously reminded himself of the steps he had taken to overcome challenges before—whether it was breaking problems down into smaller steps or working through practice problems.

On exam day, Chris walked in with a calm focus. His score reflected not only his improvement in mathematics but also his newfound confidence in his ability to reflect, regulate, and approach challenges differently. This moment was a powerful reminder to both Chris and me of the incredible impact reflection has—not just on academic results but on how students view their own potential.

Transforming Challenges into Growth Opportunities

Throughout my career, I have embraced the perspective that challenges are opportunities for growth, resonating with the encouragement in Joshua 1:9. When our district faced the implementation of a new curriculum, many educators felt overwhelmed by the changes. I encouraged them to view this transition as a chance to grow.

In our weekly meetings, we discussed the hurdles we faced and how to overcome them. Educators began sharing their reflections on what strategies worked and what didn't. This collaborative approach fostered resilience and adaptability, transforming what could have been a difficult transition into a rich learning experience for all involved.

Metacognition and Impact on Learning Outcomes

Inspiring Quote: "Challenges are what make life interesting, and overcoming them is what makes life meaningful."—Joshua J. Marine

Building a Culture of Reflective Collaboration

Creating a culture of collaboration is vital in any educational environment. I have learned that when educators share their reflective practices, it nurtures an atmosphere where feedback and growth are valued. During professional learning communities, I made it a point to encourage teachers to openly share their reflections on their teaching practices.

One department head embraced this idea, regularly leading reflective discussions during team meetings. This practice created a safe space for teachers to share insights and constructive feedback, ultimately strengthening our collective commitment to continuous improvement.

Challenge: I challenge each educator to create a "reflection journal" to document their teaching practices, successes, and areas for improvement. At the end of each week, take a few moments to review these reflections and identify patterns and opportunities for growth.

Embracing Metacognition for Lifelong Growth

The concept of metacognition empowers both educators and learners to cultivate a mindset of adaptability, resilience, and continuous growth. By reflecting on our practices and encouraging others to do the same, we refine our approaches and enhance our impact within our educational communities.

Inspiring Quote: "Education is the most powerful weapon which you can use to change the world."—Nelson Mandela.

Leadership Reflection – The Shift Is Worth It

I've seen metacognition transform entire teams. Once people start thinking about their thinking—individually and together—it changes culture. You move from defense to ownership. From blame to adjustment. From static leadership to evolving influence.

Faith Integration – "Walk by the Spirit . . ." (Galatians 5:25)

Scripture reminds us that leadership is not only about what we know, but how we live it out. *"Since we live by the Spirit, let us keep in step with the Spirit."* True reflection leads us to align our thoughts and actions with God's Spirit, moving from awareness into intentional, Spirit-led practice.

Metacognitive Leadership Asks:

- How is the Spirit guiding my thoughts and decisions in this moment?
- In what ways am I resisting His direction?
- How can I realign my leadership to reflect Christ more fully?

Reflection Prompts:

1. Where do I see evidence that my leadership flows from Spirit-led reflection rather than impulse?

2. What is one area where I need to slow down, listen, and invite God's wisdom before acting?
3. How can I demonstrate Spirit-guided reflection in a way that strengthens trust within my team?

As we integrate metacognitive practices into our leadership, we pave the way for a generation of learners who are not only knowledgeable but also equipped to navigate the complexities of the world with wisdom and purpose. Prioritizing self-awareness and reflection is essential as we strive for excellence in our educational practices.

In conclusion, integrating metacognition into our teaching and leadership practices holds tremendous potential for enhancing learning outcomes. By fostering environments that emphasize self-reflection, collaboration, and growth, we cultivate the "good treasure" within each individual.

Final Challenge: Consider how you can implement metacognitive strategies in your life, leadership, classroom, or school environment. Identify one area where you can encourage self-reflection among students or staff and take actionable steps to integrate this practice. This transformation is crucial not only for personal growth but also for meeting the challenges of today's educational landscape, ensuring that every learner has the opportunity to thrive.

Metacognition isn't just a strategy—it's a shift in how we lead, learn, and live.

Reflect. Study. Grow. Then do it again.

Chapter 10
Ethical Considerations of Metacognition in Leadership

"Integrity is doing the right thing, even when no one is watching." — C.S. Lewis

Why Ethics and Reflection Must Go Together

Metacognition helps leaders think more clearly. Ethics ensures they act more rightly.

As leaders, we bear a significant responsibility not only for our own growth but also for fostering the development of others. In this context, metacognition—the awareness and understanding of one's own thought processes—plays a crucial role. It equips leaders to make informed decisions, model reflective practices, and create an environment that encourages continuous learning and ethical behavior. When leaders reflect deeply on their decisions, motives, and actions, they develop more than skill—they build **character**. Without ethical grounding, even the most intelligent leaders can drift into self-justification, bias, and unaccountable behavior.

This chapter explores how metacognition serves as a moral compass, helping leaders discern right from wrong, humility from pride, and conviction from convenience.

Real-Life Example – Decision at a Crossroads

Years ago, I was faced with a decision as a school leader that appeared minor on the surface but carried long-term implications. A staff member I respected had crossed a line—not maliciously, but clearly—and I knew addressing it would create tension.

I wrestled.

I replayed conversations. I examined motives—both theirs and mine. I prayed. I reflected. And I asked myself the question that ultimately clarified the choice:

"If I don't address this now, what does that say about my leadership tomorrow?"

That decision, though difficult, deepened trust across the staff. People didn't agree with everything—but they saw consistency, courage, and care. That's what ethical leadership looks like when filtered through reflection.

Historical Example – Dietrich Bonhoeffer

Bonhoeffer, a German pastor during WWII, faced enormous ethical challenges under the Nazi regime. His reflection led him to join a resistance movement, costing him his life.

He once wrote, "Action springs not from thought, but from a readiness for responsibility."

That's ethical metacognition: not just thinking, but owning decisions with conviction.

Ethical Decision-Making: A Personal Reflection

One of the most challenging moments of my leadership came when I had to make a difficult ethical decision regarding a church leader's misconduct. Instead of rushing to judgment, I paused and reflected on my own values and the ethical principles that should guide my decision. This reflection allowed me to approach the situation with both fairness and compassion, balancing accountability with grace.

As a pastor, I had to navigate a delicate situation involving a respected church leader who had been accused of misconduct. Initially, I was overwhelmed by the need to act quickly, fearing the impact the scandal might have on the community. However, before making any decisions, I decided to reflect on the values that I held dear—honesty, transparency, fairness, and compassion. It was essential to approach the situation not just out of a desire to protect the church's reputation, but also to support the individual involved, who was facing their own personal turmoil.

I took time to reflect on how best to engage the situation, considering both the impact of my decision on the community and the grace needed for the individual involved. This reflective pause allowed me to make a decision that was guided by empathy, fairness, and ethical consistency. Instead of rushing to judgment, I created a process that was inclusive, providing the church leader an opportunity to express their side while ensuring accountability was maintained.

In *Dare to Lead*, Brené Brown discusses the importance of ethical leadership and the need for leaders to reflect on their values in decision-making. By using metacognitive practices, I was able to navigate a complex ethical issue with clarity, ensuring that my decisions were aligned with my values and the best interests of the community.

Reflective Leadership in Education: A Teacher's Journey

Reflecting on this experience from my pastoral leadership, I can recall a similar challenge in my role as an educational leader. During a particularly challenging school year, I became aware that one of my teachers, a highly respected individual, had been struggling with both personal and professional challenges. Despite their deep commitment to the students, it was evident that their performance was beginning to suffer. Students were feeling the impact, and the teacher's well-being seemed to be deteriorating. My initial reaction was one of concern and frustration, especially considering the teacher's history of excellent performance and leadership in the classroom.

At first, I considered addressing the issue quickly—perhaps recommending a change in responsibilities or even considering a temporary leave. But as I reflected on the situation, I realized that making such decisions out of haste, without deeper consideration of the teacher's needs, would not be ethical or in the best interest of the teacher or the students. I needed to pause and think critically about my next steps.

This is where the practice of metacognition became crucial. Instead of acting impulsively, I took time to reflect on the values I held as an educator and leader—empathy, support, fairness, and the desire to empower others. I reached out to the teacher in a private, confidential

Ethical Considerations of Metacognition in Leadership

setting, asking open-ended questions to gain insight into the challenges they were facing. I listened deeply to their struggles, both in their personal life and their classroom, and began to understand the root causes of the issues they were encountering.

This process of reflective listening and thoughtful dialogue led me to a deeper realization: the teacher needed more than just a change of assignment or a temporary fix. They needed support, not just from me as their leader but from the entire school community. Through metacognitive reflection, I came to understand that my responsibility was to model ethical leadership by taking the time to help this individual grow, rather than simply correcting their deficiencies.

I created a tailored plan for support that included mentoring, ongoing professional development, and counseling resources. Additionally, I organized a team of teachers who had expertise in the areas where the teacher was struggling to collaborate on strategies for improvement. By creating an environment that fostered reflection and growth, we were able to not only support the teacher but also strengthen the overall teaching community. I kept the lines of communication open, encouraging the teacher to reflect on their progress and helping them celebrate small victories along the way.

Over the course of the year, the teacher's performance improved, but perhaps more importantly, their confidence and well-being were restored. The process of reflection—both for myself and for the teacher—was what ultimately led to the most positive outcome. By applying metacognition, I made a decision that wasn't just based on the immediate circumstances but was rooted in a long-term, ethical approach to leadership.

The Importance of Metacognition in Leadership

Metacognition is essential for effective leadership, as it enables us to:

- **Enhance Self-Awareness:** Understanding our thought processes and decision-making strategies allows us to lead with greater clarity and purpose. I have personally experienced the value of self-reflection in my leadership journey. After a particularly challenging school year, I took time to reflect on my decisions and interactions with staff. This reflection led me to recognize areas where I could improve my communication and support, ultimately enhancing my effectiveness as a leader.

- **Model Reflective Practices:** Ethical leaders demonstrate the importance of reflection to their teams. By openly sharing my own reflective practices with my staff, I encourage them to engage in metacognition. For example, I initiated regular feedback sessions where teachers could discuss their instructional strategies and outcomes. This practice not only fostered a culture of openness but also empowered teachers to take ownership of their professional growth.

- **Encourage Continuous Improvement:** Metacognition promotes a growth mindset within educational settings. By embracing the idea that learning is an ongoing process, we can create an environment where both educators and students feel comfortable taking risks and learning from their mistakes. In one instance, after observing a lesson that didn't go as planned, I encouraged the teacher to reflect on what went well and what could be improved. This led to a valuable discussion about innovative teaching methods that ultimately benefited our students.

Key Ethical Considerations for Metacognitive Leadership

- **Fostering an Inclusive Environment:** Ethical leaders must create spaces where all voices are heard and valued. By encouraging metacognitive discussions, we can ensure that diverse perspectives contribute to our decision-making processes. During a recent curriculum review, I facilitated a series of workshops where teachers could express their insights and concerns. By incorporating their feedback into our final decisions, we not only honored their expertise but also promoted an inclusive and collaborative environment.

- **Promoting Accountability:** Metacognitive practices encourage accountability among leaders and their teams. When we reflect on our decisions and their impacts, we are more likely to take responsibility for our actions. In my experience, after implementing a new policy that initially faced resistance, I invited feedback from staff on its effectiveness. By reflecting on their input and making necessary adjustments, we were able to foster a culture of trust and accountability.

- **Encouraging Ethical Decision-Making:** Metacognition can guide leaders in making ethical choices. By reflecting on the potential consequences of our decisions, we can better align our actions with our values. I remember a time when I was faced with a difficult staffing decision. By taking a step back and considering the implications for both the individuals involved and the broader school community, I was able to make a more informed and compassionate choice.

- **Cultivating Lifelong Learning:** As leaders, we must model the importance of lifelong learning for our teams. Encouraging metacognitive practices not only enhances our own growth but also inspires others to engage in continuous self-improvement. I have found that establishing a culture of reflective practice through peer observations and shared learning an atmosphere where growth is normalized, feedback is welcomed, and learning becomes a shared journey rather than an individual task.

Faith Integration – "Who May Ascend the Hill of the Lord?" (Psalm 24:3–4)

"The one who has clean hands and a pure heart . . ."

Spiritual leadership demands both **outward integrity and inward reflection**. God does not call us to success without soul—but to walk in humility, holiness, and wisdom.

Ethical Drift Happens Slowly

Unethical behavior in leadership rarely starts with a major scandal. It starts with:

- Small rationalizations
- Lack of reflection

Ethical Considerations of Metacognition in Leadership

- Avoiding accountability
- Valuing results over people

Metacognitive leaders pause to examine:

- Why am I doing this?
- What narrative am I telling myself?
- Who might be affected by this decision?

Common Ethical Pitfalls in Leadership

- **Self-deception:** "It's not a big deal."
- **Selective accountability:** Only allowing certain people to challenge us.
- **Unquestioned ambition:** When drive overrides discernment.
- **Echo chambers:** Surrounding ourselves with affirmation, not truth.

*Metacognition guards against these by helping leaders **slow down** and examine their blind spots.*

Visual – The Ethical Reflection Loop

THE ETHICAL
REFLECTION LOOP

This loop prevents ethical drift. It keeps the leader in a **cycle of integrity**:

- **Awareness:** Recognize moral dimensions in decisions.
- **Discernment:** Weigh choices against truth and values.
- **Action:** Choose courageously.
- **Accountability:** Invite feedback and oversight.
- **Renewal:** Restore energy and perspective before the next cycle.
- *Create an atmosphere where everyone is motivated to grow together.*

Team Reflection – "The Mirror Meeting"

Schedule a staff conversation that asks only one question:

> Where in our organization are we drifting from what we value?

It's not a blame session. It's a mirror session. It opens doors for course correction, restoration, and renewed vision.

Scripture for Ethical Clarity

- **Proverbs 4:25–27:** *"Let your eyes look straight ahead . . . do not swerve to the right or the left."*
- **Micah 6:8:** *"Act justly, love mercy, and walk humbly with your God."*
- **James 3:17:** *"The wisdom from above is pure, peace-loving, gentle, reasonable, full of mercy . . ."*

Ethical leadership is not only wise—it is holy.

Reflection Questions

1. When was the last time I made an uncomfortable but ethically right decision?
2. Who in my life can tell me the truth when I'm drifting?
3. What spiritual or metacognitive habits keep me grounded in integrity?

✅ Practical Applications

1. Schedule Monthly Ethics Check-ins – Use 15–30 minutes monthly to reflect on recent decisions through a moral and spiritual lens.

2. Build an Accountability Circle – Identify 2–3 people who can challenge your motives and provide honest feedback on your leadership choices.

3. Journal Your Ethical Dilemmas – Whenever you face a tough call, document what you did, why, and what Scripture or values guided you.

4. Pause Before Rationalizing – Create a habit of asking, "What story am I telling myself—and is it true?"

✅ Reflection and Renewal

Ethical leadership begins not in rules, but in spiritual reflection. We cannot walk with integrity if we avoid asking hard questions or inviting the Holy Spirit to search our hearts.

> *"Search me, O God, and know my heart; test me and know my anxious thoughts."* —Psalm 139:23

Every decision is an opportunity to align leadership with God's character. Renewal starts with humility and honesty before the Lord.

✅ Final Thoughts

Your greatest leadership isn't measured in wins—it's measured in faithfulness to what is right.

Ethical Considerations of Metacognition in Leadership

Metacognition helps you lead with eyes wide open—not just toward results, but toward righteousness.

Lead not just with wisdom, but with a clean heart.

In navigating the complexities of educational leadership, the ethical considerations of metacognition must remain at the forefront of our practices. By fostering self-awareness, modeling reflective practices, encouraging continuous improvement, and promoting accountability, we create a nurturing environment where all individuals can thrive.

Metacognition empowers us to lead with intention and integrity, ultimately enriching the educational experiences of our students and staff. As we embrace the reflective journey of leadership, let us remember that our choices can inspire a culture of growth, collaboration, and ethical decision-making.

✓ Reflection Questions

1. What recent decision challenged my integrity or clarity of values?
2. Who in my life is trusted to ask me hard questions—and do I truly listen?
3. Where am I most tempted to rationalize instead of reflect?

✓ Team Activity – The Ethics Mirror

Objective: Encourage a culture of reflection, transparency, and integrity.

1. Ask team members to anonymously submit ethical "gray zones" they've encountered (past or present).

2. Choose 2–3 examples and facilitate a group discussion using these questions:

   - What's the right thing to do—and why?
   - How does faith or core values shape our response?
   - What would reflect long-term trust, not short-term ease?

3. Close by reading Micah 6:8 and praying for courage and clarity in leadership.

By integrating metacognitive practices into our leadership approach, we can cultivate a new generation of learners who are not only knowledgeable but also equipped to navigate the challenges of the world with wisdom and purpose. Together, let us strive to be leaders who reflect, evolve, and lead with a commitment to ethical principles that uplift and empower those we serve.

*The highest calling of leadership isn't influence—it's **integrity**.*

Metacognition sharpens our vision. Ethics strengthens our character. Together, they form a leadership that reflects God's truth and transforms others.

Reflect. Examine. Lead with integrity.

Chapter 11

Reflect, Evolve, and Lead

"We do not learn from experience . . . we learn from reflecting on experience."—John Dewey

As we navigate toward the conclusion of this exploration into metacognition and its critical role in education and leadership, it is imperative to reflect on the insights gained throughout this journey. The themes of "Reflect, Evolve, and Lead" resonate deeply, emphasizing the transformative power of reflection in fostering growth, adaptability, and effective leadership.

Throughout my life, I've seen how reflection and evolution have shaped my leadership style. Whether leading a congregation through a challenging transition or guiding a team through a complex educational initiative, I've witnessed firsthand the transformative power of metacognition. Reflecting on our leadership, our choices, and our growth allows us to evolve into more effective leaders.

John Maxwell often writes about the importance of leading with vision and purpose. He emphasizes that leaders who reflect and evolve are better equipped to guide others through change. By practicing metacognition, leaders can evolve in ways that empower those they lead.

The Journey of a Leader Begins in the Mind

You've made it through the heart of this book—not just as a reader, but as a leader actively reshaping how you think, respond, and grow. By now, you've seen that **reflection is more than a pause**—it's a power source. You've learned that **evolving isn't drifting**—it's adapting with intention. And you've discovered that **leadership isn't about control**—it's about cultivating the people and systems entrusted to you.

Now, we bring it all together.

The REL Framework: Reflect → Evolve → Lead

This simple yet powerful cycle is the heart of metacognitive leadership. When practiced intentionally, it produces sustainable growth—for individuals, teams, and organizations.

Reflect

Ask: Where am I?

- Pause.
- Look inward and upward.
- Evaluate your motives, emotions, systems, and results.

Evolve

Ask: What needs to change?

- Adapt your mindset.
- Shift strategies.
- Let God refine you through discomfort and discovery.

Lead

Ask: How will I act?

- Make decisions with courage and clarity.
- Support others.
- Build systems that reflect your values.

Then do it again.

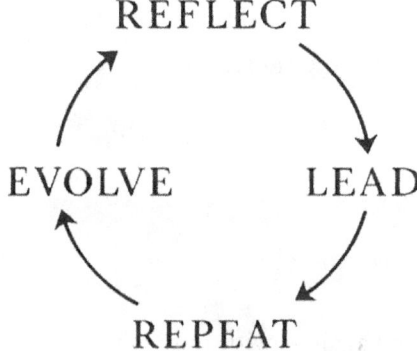

The REL Cycle

This framework isn't linear—it's dynamic and lifelong.
Every challenge invites a new level of reflection.

Every breakthrough requires new evolution.
Every season brings new leadership demands.

I didn't write this book because I figured leadership out.
I wrote it because I didn't.

Because even after decades of leading in churches, schools, and teams, I kept running into the same wall: Doing more didn't always lead to being better.

- It was **reflection** that helped me see my blind spots.
- It was **evolution** that helped me realign with what mattered.
- It was **metacognitive leadership** that changed not just my work but my heart.

If you've ever felt stuck, discouraged, unclear, or stretched too thin—I've been there. And I want you to hear this:
You don't have to stay there.

- You can pause.
- You can reflect.
- You can evolve.

And you can lead again—with purpose, peace, and power.

A Story of Reflection and Leadership Evolution

Several years ago, I was leading a church during a time of great turmoil. The congregation had grown rapidly, but we were facing significant challenges in how to maintain a sense of community and shared vision. The church was splitting in many directions, and the team was divided over several key decisions—some practical, some spiritual. The growth had been exciting, but it had also led to confusion and a loss of cohesion.

I remember waking up one morning, sitting at my kitchen table with my coffee, feeling the weight of the responsibility I carried. In my heart, I knew something had to change. I could not continue leading in a way that merely reacted to challenges, hoping they would resolve themselves. This was a time for deep reflection. As I sat there in silence, I began to reflect on my leadership journey. I thought about my mentors, the lessons I'd learned from my own failures, and the teachings I had studied about leadership in Scripture. I recalled the wise words from the Apostle Paul: "I do not consider that I have made it my own. But one thing I do: forgetting what lies behind and straining forward to what lies ahead, I press on . . ." (Philippians 3:13-14).

I had to forget the past mistakes and take an honest look at where I stood in that moment, as a leader who needed to evolve. I realized that the challenges the church faced were not only external but internal as well. The tension I was feeling was also a reflection of my leadership style—too reactive and not proactive enough in fostering a unified vision. I asked myself, "What can I do differently to guide this church with clarity and purpose?"

The next step was strategic. I decided to meet with the elders and key leaders within the church, not as a top-down authority, but as a fellow servant, asking for their input, listening intently to their concerns, and reflecting on their feedback. This process wasn't easy. Many of the leaders were disheartened and felt unheard, while others struggled with their own areas of growth. However, through honest conversation, a new vision began to emerge—a vision that was born not from one person's idea, but through collective reflection.

We devised a new strategy for the church that focused on rebuilding relationships, fostering collaboration, and most importantly, embracing a long-term vision rather than reacting to short-term problems. We introduced regular reflection periods where the leadership team could come together, share what was working, identify what needed improvement, and adjust our approaches as necessary. This shift in our leadership approach allowed us to see immediate improvements in our church community. The divisions began to heal as we grew stronger through collective reflection and intentional action.

Reflecting on that experience, I now realize that the success we achieved wasn't just about making changes to the church's programs or ministry style; it was about leading with purpose, adjusting to the evolving needs of the congregation, and embracing a culture of reflection and evolution in leadership. As I look back on that season, it's clear that the transformative power of metacognition—not just as a personal practice but as a shared process among leaders—was the key to guiding us through this difficult transition.

Faith Integration – Romans 12:2 Revisited

"Be transformed by the renewing of your mind . . ."

God's path for transformation always begins in the inner life. Let this be your leadership prayer:

- Lord, show me where I need to reflect.
- Help me evolve in character, not just competency.
- Teach me to lead from overflow—not exhaustion.

Team Exercise – The REL Huddle

Use this structure weekly or monthly with your leadership team:

- **Reflect:** What's one insight you've gained this week?
- **Evolve:** What's one habit or perspective you're working on?

- **Lead:** How will you bring this change into your work or team?

Over time, this rhythm will transform your team's culture.

The Essence of Reflective Practice

Reflective practice is at the heart of effective education and leadership. It involves the conscious consideration of one's actions, thoughts, and experiences, allowing individuals to assess their effectiveness and make informed adjustments. This chapter aims to recap the key insights we have explored, weaving them back into the themes of reflection and evolution in leadership.

- **The Power of Reflection:** Reflection empowers educators and leaders to take ownership of their practices. By regularly examining their experiences, they can identify areas for improvement and celebrate successes. For example, as a school leader, I recall implementing a new curriculum initiative that initially faced resistance. Through reflective discussions with my team, we recognized the need for additional training and support, which ultimately led to successful implementation. This experience taught us that reflection is not just a personal endeavor but a collaborative one that fosters a culture of continuous improvement.
- **Cultivating a Growth Mindset:** Embracing a growth mindset is crucial for evolving as an educator and leader. By viewing challenges as opportunities for growth, individuals can develop resilience and adaptability. I witnessed this firsthand during a professional development workshop

where educators shared their struggles and triumphs. The open dialogue encouraged vulnerability, allowing participants to learn from one another and grow collectively. This environment of shared reflection is essential for building strong, adaptive teams that can navigate the complexities of education.

- **Empowering Others through Reflection:** As leaders, our role is to empower others to reflect on their practices. By modeling reflective behavior, we create a safe space for educators and students to engage in self-assessment. A poignant example comes from my experience working with a mentor teacher who implemented reflective journaling in her classroom. This practice not only helped her students articulate their learning experiences but also encouraged them to take risks and learn from their mistakes. Empowering others through reflection fosters a sense of ownership over their learning and growth.

Metacognition as a Leadership Imperative

As we embrace the theme of leadership, it becomes clear that metacognition is fundamental to effective leadership. Understanding one's thinking processes allows leaders to navigate challenges with clarity and purpose. Here are some key aspects of how metacognition serves as a pillar of leadership:

- **Self-Awareness:** Leaders who practice metacognition are more self-aware, recognizing their strengths and areas for growth. This awareness fosters humility and the willingness to seek feedback, ultimately leading to better decision-making. Reflecting on past experiences as a leader, I have learned to appreciate constructive criticism, which has enhanced my ability to lead effectively.

- **Strategic Thinking:** Metacognition encourages strategic thinking, enabling leaders to analyze situations, evaluate options, and make informed decisions. For instance, during a crisis in our district, I utilized metacognitive strategies to assess our response. By reflecting on previous challenges and outcomes, I was able to devise a plan that prioritized communication and collaboration among staff and stakeholders.

- **Fostering a Culture of Reflection:** Leaders who prioritize metacognition create a culture of reflection within their organizations. By encouraging team members to engage in reflective practices, leaders cultivate an environment that values continuous improvement and collaboration. For example, implementing regular reflective team meetings allows staff to share insights and strategies, fostering a community of learners committed to evolving together.

Embracing the Future

As we conclude this exploration, let us embrace the future with a commitment to reflection, evolution, and leadership. The journey of education is a continuous cycle of learning and growth, where reflective practices serve as the foundation for effective leadership. By prioritizing metacognitive strategies, we can equip ourselves and our teams to navigate the complexities of education with confidence and clarity.

In our roles as educators and leaders, let us remain dedicated to the ideals of lifelong learning, adaptability, and critical thinking. Together, we can create educational environments that empower individuals to thrive, embracing the beauty of each season in our professional journeys. As we reflect on our experiences and evolve in our practices, we position ourselves to lead with wisdom and purpose, shaping a brighter future for all learners.

Closing Charge

You are not called to be perfect. You are called to be **faithful, thoughtful, and teachable**. The world doesn't need more reactive leaders.

It needs more **reflective leaders** who evolve and lead with purpose.

So wherever you go next—
Whatever challenge arises—
Remember this:

Reflect. Evolve. Lead.

Then do it again.

Chapter 12

Metacognition: Shaping the Future of Learning and Leadership

"To be able to be caught up into the world of thought, that is being educated." —Edith Hamilton

It is time to look beyond the immediate and cast our vision toward the horizon. The power of metacognition reaches far beyond the confines of classrooms—it is a transformative force that shapes not just how we learn, but how we adapt, lead, and inspire. Through deep self-awareness, intentional reflection, and thoughtful action, metacognition holds the key to a future driven by continuous growth, adaptability, and purpose. In this chapter, we will explore the powerful insights gained through our journey, envision a future where metacognitive practices shape our world, and outline the steps educators and leaders must take to create an environment where reflection, adaptability, and growth are not only encouraged but thrive.

Metacognition is more than a personal tool—it is a cornerstone of transformational leadership and education. Over the years, in my journey as a pastor, educator, and leader, I have witnessed firsthand the profound impact of metacognitive awareness. I've seen how leaders who can reflect on their own thinking create change that extends far beyond their own growth to shape communities, organizations, and the lives of those they serve. One of the most powerful examples occurred when I began mentoring young leaders in the church. As I guided them to reflect critically on their decision-making and personal biases, I saw them grow into more thoughtful, self-aware, and effective leaders—ones who made decisions not only with wisdom but with a sense of higher purpose.

A New Kind of Leader for a New Kind of World

We are living in one of the most dynamic, disruptive, and opportunity-rich periods in history. In this moment, the most effective leaders won't be those who simply know more or move faster. They will be those who can **think about how they think**, evolve with purpose, and lead with deep reflection.

Metacognition is not just a skill. It's a **paradigm** that will shape the future of leadership, learning, and human development.

What the Future Needs

Future-ready leaders must:

- Reflect honestly, even under pressure
- Evolve wisely, even amidst uncertainty
- Lead humbly, even in the spotlight

They must create systems and cultures that:

- Foster self-awareness in every layer of the organization
- Promote feedback and reflection as part of the process
- Develop others to lead themselves—not just follow well

My Vision – Leading Through the Lens of Reflection

As a leader, I don't want to produce rule followers—I want to develop **reflective thinkers** who know how to grow when no one's watching.

As a spiritual influencer, I don't want a crowd that only listens—I want people who **examine themselves**, align with God, and walk in truth.

As a father and mentor, I've learned that the future isn't built by control but by **cultivating metacognition** in others: helping them reflect, adapt, and lead.

I believe metacognitive leadership will be **the defining trait of transformational influence** in the decades ahead.

A Journey through Challenges and Reflection: A Story of Growth

Several years ago, I found myself in the midst of a challenging situation that required deep reflection—both from me as a leader and from those I was leading. In my role as a pastor, I was tasked with overseeing a church that had grown increasingly divided. The disagreements among staff and congregation members had become more pronounced, and a sense of disunity was creeping into the very fabric of the church's mission. As I stood at the helm of the organization, I realized that the traditional methods of leadership—those based solely on authority and knowledge—would no longer suffice. What I needed was a vision grounded in reflection, adaptability, and trust.

I turned to the very principles of metacognition that I had spent years cultivating in my own leadership practices. I asked myself questions: How had I contributed to the division? What assumptions had I made about my role as a leader and the needs of my congregation? How had I failed to listen and adapt to the changing dynamics around me?

It was during this period of deep self-reflection that I recognized a fundamental truth: True leadership requires the humility to admit when one's approach is no longer effective. I began to share my reflections openly with my team, modeling the vulnerability that Brené Brown so powerfully describes in *Dare to Lead*. In doing so, I not only empowered my leaders to engage in their own reflective practices but also created a space where the team could unite around a shared vision—one that valued learning from past mistakes and growing together.

The journey was not without its challenges, but as we collectively embraced a culture of reflection, we began to see the fruit of our efforts. Disagreements turned into thoughtful discussions, and mistrust gave way to collaboration. The church, once fragmented, began to function as a cohesive body once again. This experience reinforced my belief in the transformative power of metacognitive leadership—leadership that encourages reflection not only in oneself but also within the team, fostering an environment where growth and adaptability can flourish.

Shaping a Future with Metacognitive Leadership

John Maxwell, in *The 21 Irrefutable Laws of Leadership*, emphasizes the power of vision in leadership: A leader must see beyond the immediate and inspire others to do the same. This is where metacognitive skills come in: Leaders who can anticipate future challenges and opportunities can more effectively shape the future. I've experienced this firsthand in my leadership roles, where reflecting on the long-term implications of decisions helped me craft a vision for the future of both the church and the school district I served. Metacognition helped me adjust my strategies, navigate complex challenges, and ensure I was always prepared for the future.

Brené Brown builds on this concept by highlighting the importance of vulnerability and reflection in leadership. Leaders who are willing to reflect on their assumptions, engage in vulnerability, and learn from their mistakes foster trust, creativity, and innovation in their teams. As education and leadership continue to evolve, those who embrace metacognitive practices—leaders who engage in deep reflection—will be the ones who succeed. By shaping the future of learning and leadership with intentional reflection, we can create environments that encourage growth, ethical decision-making, and transformative change.

In my experience, the future of leadership depends on empowering others with metacognitive skills. Whether in the church, the classroom, or the workplace, fostering a culture of reflection is vital. As leaders, we must teach the next generation to think critically about their thinking, helping them develop a deeper understanding of themselves and the world around them.

Key Insights from Our Journey

1. **The Power of Self-Awareness in Learning and Growth**

    At the heart of metacognition is the ability to understand one's own thoughts, strengths, and limitations. This self-awareness empowers both learners and leaders to navigate their journeys with purpose and clarity. When learners reflect on their study habits and outcomes, they are able to adapt and refine their strategies. Similarly, when leaders engage in reflective practice, they become aware of their impact on others, fostering environments that promote openness, growth, and continuous improvement.

Example: One high school student, struggling in math, initially faced a steep learning curve. Through guided reflection with her teacher, she recognized her strength in visual learning. By incorporating visual aids and practice problems into her study routine, she not only improved her grades but grew in confidence. Her journey illustrates the profound impact of metacognitive awareness on unlocking potential.

2. **Empowerment through Reflective Practices**

    When educators model reflective practices, they foster a culture of metacognition that empowers students and staff alike. Reflection becomes a habit—a way of thinking that leads to resilience, adaptability, and a commitment to continuous growth. In classrooms and organizations where reflective practice is embraced, both successes and setbacks become valuable opportunities for learning and improvement.

    Example: A principal I once worked with introduced "Reflection Fridays," encouraging staff to pause and reflect on the week. This practice created a culture of openness and support, transforming the school environment into one that thrived on shared growth and collaboration.

3. **Lifelong Learning and Adaptability**

   As the world of education evolves, those who embrace metacognition are better equipped to adapt. Self-assessment, goal-setting, and reflection help individuals develop resilience and a proactive mindset. These practices empower leaders and learners to navigate change with curiosity, flexibility, and an openness to learning.

   Example: In today's digital age, a teacher who regularly assesses her approach to technology ensures she remains at the forefront of effective teaching. By reflecting on what works and what could be improved, she creates a more dynamic and engaging learning environment—illustrating the lifelong benefits of metacognitive practices.

Future Directions for Metacognitive Education and Leadership

As we look ahead, several pathways will drive the integration of metacognition into education and leadership:

1. **Innovative Teaching Practices**

   Educators should prioritize metacognitive strategies in their teaching, encouraging students to set goals, self-monitor, and reflect on their learning processes. By giving students ownership over their learning, we cultivate a deeper sense of purpose and engagement.

   Example: In one district, teachers introduced "Reflection Pauses" mid-lesson, where students would write down what they had learned and what questions remained. This small practice led to increased engagement and accountability, with students becoming more active participants in their learning journey.

2. **Professional Development for Educators**

   To embed metacognitive practices effectively, educators need ongoing professional development. Programs focused on reflection and metacognition can equip teachers with the tools to transform their teaching and the learning culture in their classrooms.

   Example: A district-wide series of workshops focused on metacognitive strategies empowered educators to guide students in setting personal goals and reflecting on their progress. The result was increased motivation and clearer learning goals among students.

3. **Building Collaborative Learning Environments**

   Collaboration fosters shared reflection and the exchange of ideas, amplifying metacognitive growth. When students and staff engage in meaningful conversations about their learning experiences, they broaden their perspectives and deepen their understanding.

   Example: A middle school math teacher implemented "Partner Reflections" where students worked together to review what strategies had worked for them and where they had struggled. This collaborative practice helped create a supportive, growth-oriented learning environment.

Research and Evaluation

Ongoing research into the effectiveness of metacognitive practices will guide their future implementation. By studying the impact of these practices in diverse educational settings, we can develop evidence-based strategies that benefit learners across contexts.

The Future-Focused Leader's Framework

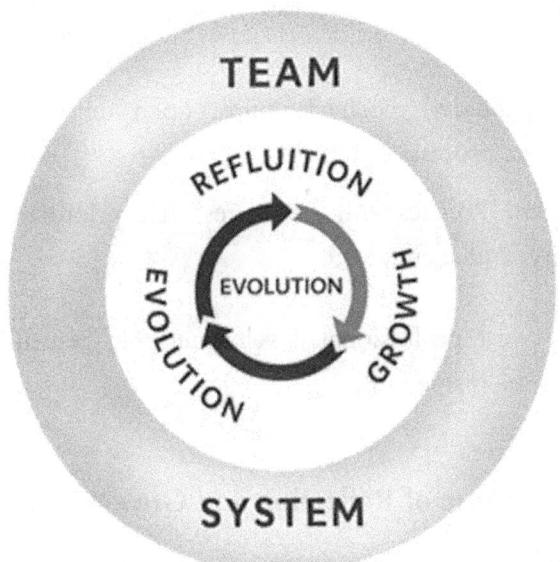

I'd like to introduce "refluition" as a signature concept in this book. I see it as more than just a word—it's a framework that ties together the heart of *Reflect, Evolve, Lead.*

Here's how I define it:

Refluition (n.): *The intentional process of reflection, evolution, and action in leadership. It is the cycle of pausing to reflect, evolving in thought and practice, and moving forward with renewed clarity and purpose.*

Refluition is the process of reflecting deeply on one's actions, evolving in thought and practice, and then leading with renewed clarity and purpose. It is the cycle of pause, growth, and forward movement that transforms leaders and those they serve.

- **Individual:** Self-awareness, reflection routines, moral clarity
- **Team:** Shared feedback loops, open reflection spaces, adaptive processes
- **System:** Policies and structures that prioritize growth, equity, and agency

This isn't just professional development. It's **cultural development**—from the inside out.

Creating a Culture of Reflection and Growth

Institutional leaders must champion reflection as a cornerstone of continuous improvement. By creating environments that value self-awareness and growth, we build communities that recognize learning as a journey, not a destination.

A Call to Action: Embracing the Future of Metacognition

The time for transformation is now. Educators and leaders must commit to embedding metacognitive practices in meaningful ways. As we face a world that demands adaptability, reflection, and critical thinking, metacognition is the key to unlocking potential in every individual. This journey is not simply about imparting knowledge—it's about shaping individuals who think deeply, act intentionally, and navigate complexities with wisdom and compassion.

As Edith Hamilton so beautifully put it, true education lies in being "caught up in the world of thought." Together, we can harness the power of metacognition to shape a brighter, more reflective future—one where leaders, educators, and students alike continuously grow, adapt, and thrive.

Faith Integration – The Long View of Growth

Philippians 1:6 says, *"He who began a good work in you will carry it on to completion."*

God is not done growing you.
Your leadership journey is not static.
There is always more to reflect on, more to refine, more to become.
Leaders who walk with the Spirit reflect often, evolve faithfully, and lead from overflow—not exhaustion.

Reflection Questions

1. What systems or practices can I establish to keep reflection ongoing in my leadership context?
2. Who can I develop into a reflective leader who multiplies growth?
3. How can I personally commit to metacognitive growth in this next season?

The Leader's Commission

You have walked through the pages of this book. You've seen the cost of unreflective leadership and the power of thoughtful, evolving guidance.

Now, take what you've seen, and **live it.**

- Lead with integrity.
- Reflect often.
- Evolve with wisdom.

And lead—boldly, humbly, and faithfully.

- The world needs you.
- Not a perfect leader.
- But a reflective one.

One who is willing to keep growing—no matter what.

Reflect. Evolve. Lead. Then do it again.

Chapter 13

Leading Through Metacognition

A Call to Inspire, Empower, and Transform

"We lead not by commanding, but by inspiring."
—Unknown

As we close the journey of *Reflect, Evolve, Lead*, we arrive at a profound truth: Leadership that transforms lives does not stem from control, charisma, or positional authority—it grows from reflection, intentionality, and the courage to evolve. This is the heart of metacognitive leadership.

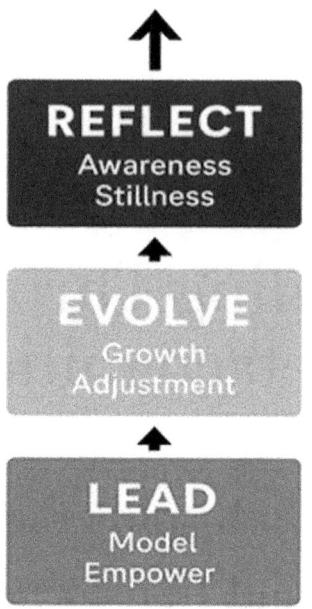

◆ Reflect

Effective leaders pause. They think deeply. They consider their motivations, decisions, reactions, and direction. Reflection is not optional—it is essential. In moments of conflict or confusion, reflection is the steady light. I recall standing alone in my office during one of my most difficult seasons of ministry and leadership. I was overwhelmed. Everything around me was demanding answers, direction, resolution. But instead of reacting, I chose to *reflect*. I asked:

- What am I truly feeling?
- What patterns are emerging?
- What does this situation reveal about me and those I lead?

In that moment, I discovered the power of stillness. Through reflection, I saw not only the problem but the pathway forward.

◆ Evolve

Leaders who reflect begin to grow. They adjust. They become more aware of their blind spots and more attuned to the needs of their people. Evolution isn't dramatic; it's often quiet. It happens in the late-night journaling, the early morning prayer, the hard conversations we replay in our minds.

One young leader I mentored struggled to make decisions without fear of failure. Instead of giving him the answers, I taught him to reflect. To pause. To ask himself what he believed, what values he held, and what outcomes mattered most. Over time, he grew—not just in confidence, but in clarity and conviction. That's the power of metacognitive evolution.

🧠 Lead

True leadership is not a performance—it's a pattern. A lifestyle. A posture of the heart. Leaders who lead metacognitively don't pretend to have all the answers. Instead, they model what it means to keep learning. They:

- Share their reflections openly
- Invite others into thoughtful dialogue
- Cultivate environments of psychological safety
- Use every setback as a setup for growth

I once introduced "reflection huddles" with my leadership team. We didn't always solve the big problems in those moments—but we always left with deeper insight, stronger bonds, and a renewed sense of shared purpose.

✴ The Metacognitive Leadership Mode

Leading through metacognition requires more than instructing others; it involves modeling the very practices of reflection, self-awareness, and growth that we wish to cultivate in those we lead. In my own leadership journey, I've witnessed how embracing metacognitive practices has allowed me to lead with greater clarity, purpose, and empathy. One particular moment stands out—a time when I worked alongside a group of church leaders during a particularly challenging period. We were facing external pressures, internal conflicts, and a shifting cultural landscape. It would have been easy to become overwhelmed, but through reflective leadership, I maintained a sense of peace and focus.

In Practice, Leading Through Metacognition Involves:

- **Modeling Reflection**: Actively reflecting on your leadership practices and sharing these reflections with your team.
- **Encouraging Self-Awareness**: Empowering those you lead to regularly assess their thought processes, decisions, and assumptions.
- **Fostering a Growth Mindset**: Cultivating a culture where mistakes are viewed as opportunities for reflection and growth, not failures.

- **Continuous Learning**: Committing to lifelong learning and using metacognitive practices to continually improve and evolve as a leader.

Through these practices, metacognition becomes not just a tool for individual growth but a foundational approach to leading others. Whether you are leading a church, school, or community organization, reflective thinking and self-awareness help create thoughtful, effective, and resilient leaders—capable of adapting to the ever-changing demands of leadership. By leading through metacognition, we shape the next generation of leaders who will navigate the complexities of their roles and make a lasting impact.

Leading through metacognition isn't simply about making decisions in the moment; it's about fostering a culture where leaders are constantly reflecting on their choices, learning from their experiences, and evolving to meet new challenges. As I reflect on my own leadership growth, I see how vital metacognition has been in shaping my approach to leading others.

Embracing Metacognitive Leadership: The Essence of Purposeful Guidance

To lead with metacognition is to embrace leadership with a mindset that values continuous learning, self-reflection, and purposeful action. Leaders who harness the power of metacognition are more than just managers—they are mentors, guiding others to recognize and activate their own potential. This type of leadership is characterized by humility, resilience, and an unwavering commitment to the growth of others. When we lead with metacognition, we model behaviors, mindsets, and reflective practices that nurture resilient, adaptive teams, ready to navigate change.

How Metacognition Transforms Leadership Practices

Reflective leaders don't strive for perfection—they value progress, insight, and growth. They see mistakes as stepping stones and challenges as opportunities for innovation. Metacognitive leaders ask:

- What can we learn from this experience?
- How can we adapt to improve future outcomes?
- What strengths did we demonstrate, and where can we refine our approach?

By asking these questions, leaders can foster a culture where reflection is second nature. This empowers teams to embrace mistakes as learning tools and reinforces a growth mindset—an essential foundation for innovation and progress.

The Impact of Reflective Leadership on Team Culture

A metacognitive leader nurtures a culture of open dialogue, empathy, and respect. Team members feel valued, seen, and heard, fostering trust that fuels collaboration and creativity. By encouraging reflective practices, leaders empower individuals to understand their unique roles in the collective mission. This mutual respect transforms organizational culture, ensuring that everyone contributes to an environment that values learning, respects diverse perspectives, and adapts with purpose.

For instance, a reflective leader might implement "reflection huddles," where teams gather to discuss recent achievements, challenges, and insights. In these huddles, each member is encouraged to share personal reflections, promoting transparency and collective growth. This simple practice can deepen trust, reinforce shared values, and amplify team resilience.

Empowering Others to Lead through Self-Awareness

Metacognitive leadership is ultimately about creating leaders at every level. When individuals are empowered to reflect, evolve, and lead, they become agents of change in their own right. A metacognitive leader fosters independence by equipping others with tools for self-reflection, self-regulation, and critical thinking.

Imagine a school where educators engage in reflective practices alongside their students, guiding them through self-assessment and goal-setting. These students, shaped by metacognitive principles, grow into resilient, thoughtful adults who understand the value of reflection. Not only do they become better learners, but they also emerge as future leaders.

A Story of Leadership Transformation: Leading Through Metacognition

In one pivotal chapter of my leadership journey, I faced a challenge that tested not only my leadership skills but the very essence of my understanding of reflective leadership. It was a time when my leadership team was on the verge of disarray. We were managing a significant change in the church, one that stirred internal conflict, and external pressures were mounting. We were no longer simply addressing day-to-day tasks; we were confronting deeply rooted concerns that challenged the core of our community's identity.

Amidst these challenges, I realized that if I led without reflection—without pausing to understand my thoughts, my fears, and my emotional responses—I risked steering the team in a direction driven by haste and panic. The first step in addressing this crisis was to reflect deeply on my own leadership. Standing alone in my office, I asked myself: *What am I missing in the way I'm currently leading?*

It was at that moment that I realized my reactive approach wasn't working. I began to shift my leadership style by inviting my team into the reflective process. Rather than solving their problems immediately, I engaged them with reflective questions: *What are you feeling? What is the true issue here? How can we align our actions with our mission's deeper values?*

In time, the transformation was remarkable. As we modeled reflection and vulnerability, the team began to mirror these behaviors, asking more insightful questions, seeking deeper understanding before reacting, and sharing reflections openly. The more we engaged in reflective practices, the more empowered we became—not just as individuals but as a collective leadership team.

The true transformation occurred when this reflective leadership began to shape our congregation. Instead of reacting with frustration, we addressed concerns with empathy and clarity. We were no longer leading from a place of fear—we were leading from insight and intentionality, making decisions that aligned with our values. This was the power of metacognitive leadership, and it became the foundation for lasting change within our community.

The Future of Metacognitive Leadership: A Call to Action

Looking toward the future, the responsibility to lead with insight and intention has never been more pressing. In a world where adaptability, emotional intelligence, and reflective thinking are indispensable, metacognitive leadership is vital. To lead metacognitively is to forge a path toward a more thoughtful, resilient, and interconnected world.

🔔 Your Call to Action

As you walk away from these pages, let this final chapter stay with you—not just in thought, but in practice:

- **Lead with Purpose** – Make decisions shaped by reflection and values, not impulse or pressure.
- **Empower with Compassion** – Invite others to think deeply, speak honestly, and grow courageously.
- **Reflect with Consistency** – Build rhythms of reflection into your leadership lifestyle.
- **Evolve with Intent** – Never stop growing. Let every experience teach you something new.
- **Model the Way** – Be the leader others want to become—not because you're perfect, but because you're *intentional*.

🧠 Final Words: Legacy through Reflection

As we close this journey through *Reflect, Evolve, Lead*, let us embrace the profound role that metacognition can play in our lives and in the lives of those we influence. May we lead with wisdom, inspire with intention, and empower with compassion, shaping a future where every individual has the tools to thrive and the insight to lead with purpose.

You are not just a leader of people—you are a multiplier of leaders, a cultivator of culture, a steward of influence. Your impact is measured not in your accomplishments alone but in the growth you foster in others. The legacy you leave will not be defined by how loud your voice was, but by how deeply your leadership helped others discover their own.

So lead with courage. Lead with awareness. Lead with humility. Lead through metacognition.
And always . . .

Reflect. Evolve. Lead.

References

Alter, A., Oppenheimer, D., Epley, N., & Eyre, R. (2007). Overcoming intuition: Metacognitive difficulty activates analytic reasoning. *Journal of Experimental Psychology, 136*(4), 569-576.

Anderson, F., & Nashon, S. (2006). Predators of knowledge construction: Interpreting students' metacognition in an amusement park physics program. Retrieved from http://www.interscience.wiley.com (DOI 10.1002/sce.20176).

August, D. L., Flavell, J. H., & Clift, R. (1984). Comparison of comprehension monitoring of skilled and less skilled readers. *Reading Research Quarterly, 20*(1), 39-54.

Borkowski, J. G. (1992). Metacognition theory: A framework for teaching literacy, writing, and math skills. *Journal of Learning Disabilities, 25*(4), 253-257.

Boulware-Gooden, R., Carreker, S., Thornhill, A., & Joshi, M. (2007). Instruction of metacognitive strategies enhances reading comprehension and vocabulary achievement of third-grade students. *The Reading Teacher, 61*(1), 70-77.

Bransford, J., Sherwood, R., Vye, N., & Rieser, J. (1986). Teaching thinking and problem solving. *American Psychologist, 41*(10), 1078-1089.

Bransford, J. D., Brown, A. L., & Cocking, R. R. (Eds.). (2000). *How people learn: Brain, mind, experience, and school.* Washington, D.C.: National Academy Press.

Brown, Brené. (2018). *Dare to Lead: Brave Work. Tough Conversations. Whole Hearts.* Random House.

- Reference to how leaders who are willing to engage in vulnerability and reflection inspire trust, creativity, and growth within their teams.
- Reference to building trust, modeling vulnerability, and creating environments where others feel safe to reflect and learn.

Case, J., & Gunstone, R. (2002). Metacognitive development as a shift in approach to learning: An in-depth study. *Studies in Higher Education, 27*(4), 459-470.

Cooper, S. (1999). Theories of learning in educational psychology: John Flavell: metacognition. Retrieved from http://www.lifecircles-inc.com/Learningtheories/constructivism/flavell.html

Costa, A., & Kallick, B. (2008). *Learning & leading with habits of mind.* New York: ASCD.

DiGisi, L., & Yore, L. D. (1992, March). Reading comprehension and metacognition in science: Status, potential and future directions. Paper presented at the National Association for Research in Science Teaching Annual Meeting. Retrieved from ERIC database (ED 356 132).

Dweck, C. (2006). *Mindset: The new psychology of success*. New York: Random House.

Everson, H. T., & Tobias, S. (1998). The ability to estimate knowledge and performance in college: A metacognitive analysis. *Instructional Science, 26*(1-2), 65-79.

Fisher, R. (1998). Thinking about thinking: Developing metacognition in children. *Early Child Development and Care, 141*(1), 1-15.

Flavell, J. H. (1979). Speculations about the nature and development of metacognition. In F. Weinert & R. Kluwe (Eds.), *Metacognition and motivation* (pp. 21-29). Hillsdale, NJ: Lawrence Erlbaum Associates.

Flavell, J. H. (1987). Metacognition and cognitive monitoring: A new era in cognitive developmental inquiry. *American Psychologist, 34*(10), 906-911.

Georghiades, P. (2004). From the general to the situated: Three decades of metacognition. *International Journal of Science Education, 26*(3), 365-383.

Glaser, R. (1984). Education and thinking: The role of knowledge. *American Psychologist, 39*(2), 93-104.

Hacker, D. J., & Dunlosky, J. (2003). Not all metacognition is created equal. *New Directions for Teaching and Learning, 95*, 73-79.

Hartman, H. J. (2001a). Developing students' metacognitive knowledge and strategies. In H. J. Hartman (Ed.), *Metacognition in learning and instruction: Theory, research, and practice* (pp. 33-68). Dordrecht, The Netherlands: Kluwer Academic Publishers.

Hartman, H. J. (2001b). Teaching metacognitively. In H. J. Hartman (Ed.), *Metacognition in learning and instruction: Theory, research, and practice* (pp. 149-169). Dordrecht, The Netherlands: Kluwer Academic Publishers.

Hartman, H. J. (2001c). Metacognition in science teaching and learning. In H. J. Hartman (Ed.), *Metacognition in learning and instruction: Theory, research, and practice* (pp. 173-201). Dordrecht, The Netherlands: Kluwer Academic Publishers.

Hobson, E. (2008, July). The role of metacognition in teaching reading comprehension. Retrieved from http://metacognition.org

Houtveen, A. A. M., & Van de Grift, J. C. M. (2007). Effects of metacognitive strategy instruction and instruction time on reading comprehension. *School Effectiveness and School Improvement, 18*(2), 173-190.

Jones, B. F., & Idol, L. (1990). Introduction. In B. F. Jones & L. Idol (Eds.), *Dimensions of thinking and cognitive instruction* (pp. 1-14). Hillsdale, NJ: Erlbaum.

Karelina, A., & Etkina, E. (2006). When and how do students engage in sense-making in a physics lab? Paper presented at the Physics Education Research Conference. American Institute of Physics. Retrieved from EBSCOHost database (978-0-7354-0383-3).

Lamport, M., & Yoder, D. (2006, Spring). Faithful gestures: Rebooting the educational mission of the church. *Christian Education Journal, 58-78.*

Larkin, J. H., & Simon, H. A. (1987). Why a diagram is (sometimes) worth a thousand words. *Cognitive Science, 11*, 65-69.

Lionni, L. (1970). *Fish is fish*. New York: Scholastic Press.

Livingston, J. A. (1997). Metacognition: An overview. Retrieved from http://gse.buffalo.edu/fas/shuell/CEP564/Metacog.htm

Maxwell, John C. (2007). *The 21 Irrefutable Laws of Leadership: Follow Them and People Will Follow You*. Thomas Nelson.

- Reference to the importance of vision in leadership and how a leader must see the bigger picture and inspire others to do the same.

Maxwell, John C. (2011). *The 5 Levels of Leadership: Proven Steps to Maximize Your Potential*. Center Street.

- Reference to the role of leaders in helping others grow and develop into better leaders.

Paris, S. G., & Winograd, P. (1990). How metacognition can promote academic learning and instruction. In B. F. Jones & L. Idol (Eds.), *Dimensions of thinking and cognitive instruction* (pp. 15-51). Hillsdale, NJ: Erlbaum.

Piaget, J. (1973). *The language and thought of the child*. London: Routledge & Kegan Paul.

Pintrich, P. R. (2002). The role of metacognitive knowledge in learning, teaching, and assessing. *Theory Into Practice, 41*(4), 219-225.

Pressley, M., Wharton-McDonald, R., Mistretta-Hampton, J., & Echevarria, M. (1998). Literacy instruction in 10 fourth-and fifth-grade classrooms in upstate New York. *Scientific Studies of Reading, 2*(2), 159-194.

Redish, E. F. (1994). The implications of cognitive studies for teaching physics. *American Journal of Physics, 62*(6), 796-803.

Roberts, M. J., & Erdos, G. (1993). Strategy selection and metacognition. *Educational Psychology, 13*(3/4), 259-266.

Salmon, A. (2008). Promoting a culture of thinking in the young child. *Early Childhood Education Journal, 35*, 457-461.

Slavin, R. S. (1980). Cooperative learning. *Review of Educational Research, 50*(2), 315-342.

Vosniadou, S., & Brewer, W. F. (1989). The concept of the earth's shape: A study of conceptual change in childhood. Unpublished paper. Center for the Study of Reading, University of Illinois, Champaign.

Vygotsky, L. S. (1978). *Mind in society: The development of the higher psychological processes.* Cambridge, MA: The Harvard University Press.

Waltke, B. (2005). *The book of Proverbs: Chapters 15-31.* Wm. B. Eerdmans.

Wall, K., & Higgins, S. (2006). Facilitating metacognitive talk: A research and learning tool. *International Journal of Research & Method in Education, 29*(1), 39-53.

Webb, N. M. (1982). Student interaction and learning in small groups. *Review of Educational Research, 52*(3), 421-445.

Weinert, F. (1987). Introduction and overview: Metacognition and motivation as determinants of effective learning and understanding. In F. Weinert & R. H. Kluwe (Eds.), *Metacognition, Motivation, and Understanding* (pp. 1-16). Hillsdale, NJ: Erlbaum.

About the Author

Dr. Teddy Ott is an author, educator, pastor, and leader with a passion for helping others grow through reflection and metacognition. He has served as a superintendent, principal, coach, and counselor, drawing on decades of leadership in education, ministry, and business. Dr. Ott has written multiple books, including *Changed*, *The Narcissistic Church*, and *The Pharisee in You*, each challenging readers to think deeply and live with purpose. He lives in Texas, where he continues to write, lead, and inspire others to reflect, evolve, and lead.

www.ingramcontent.com/pod-product-compliance
Lightning Source LLC
Chambersburg PA
CBHW060523090426
42735CB00011B/2341